MW01088415

Put Your Money Where Your Heart Is

An Easy-to-Understand Guide to Investments

Sherman S. Smith, Ph.D.

Meister Press / *Chicago*

Published in Winthrop Harbor, Illinois by Meister Press, a division of DunkMeister Communications. Requests for permission to use portions of this book may be directed to:

> Sherman S. Smith, Ph.D., Chairman
> SSS&A Investment Advisors, Inc.
> 1836 Second St. / Napa, CA 94559
> phone: 800/424-5577   FAX: 707/252-2891

For information on purchasing this book, either singly or in quantity, see page 194.

Requests for editorial and publishing services may be directed to:

> Duncan Jaenicke, President
> Meister Press / 806 Russell Ave.
> Winthrop Harbor, IL 60096
> phone & FAX: 847/872-0035

The glossary in this book is reprinted in part by permission from John Wiley & Sons. See page 193 for complete notation.

Library of Congress Cataloging-in-Publication Data

Smith, Sherman S.
    Put your money where your heart is: an easy-to-understand guide to investments /
    Sherman S. Smith
        p. cm.
    Includes bibliographical references.
    ISBN 0-9643136-1-8
    1. Investing—aspects of.   2. Business—understanding investment options.
    3. Money—how to invest. I. Title.

Printed in the United States of America

1 2 3 4 5 6 8 9

DEDICATION

To "The Bandits"

CONTENTS

PART 3: INVESTMENT VEHICLES

ACKNOWLEDGMENTS

Without the efforts of Mr. George McCuen, who is the president of our company, SSS&A Investment Advisors, Inc., this book would not have come to fruition. George labored tirelessly to write two of the chapters. His expertise is incalculable in the overall worth of what you are about to read.

I wish to thank George for taking this book on as a personal project. It is not easy to write a technical book in layman's terms. He 'held my feet to the fire' on many issues to make sure the public gets the right understanding on the various issues this book is trying to cover.

I also wish to thank my agent, editor, and friend, Duncan Jaenicke, for helping put all this together.

And thanks also go to Bob Zaloba, who helped us shape the book to best serve its audience, in the beginning days of this project.

FOREWORD

Every so often a book hits both the Christian and secular bookstores that comes under the 'must read' category. Sherman Smith's first book, *Exploding the Doomsday Money Myths—Why It's <u>Not</u> Time to Panic*, was one such monograph; his most recent effort, *Put Your Money Where Your Heart Is—An Easy-to-Understand Guide to Investments*, carries the same sound research, common sense, and Christian viewpoint.

Sherman is quickly becoming one of America's premiere financial advisors—and with good reason. His level-headed, common-sense approach to a sometimes confusing subject—investing and money in general—is a breath of fresh air in a world filled with economic predictions ranging from wild-eyed enthusiasm to ominous portents of *The End*.

In his first book, Dr. Smith was rightly indignant about the common 'doom-and-gloom' scenarios so distressingly common today in Christian prophecy and/or economic books. In a superlative manner his most recent effort, *Put Your Money Where Your Heart Is*, is an effective follow-up to his *Doomsday* tome in that he offers sound financial advice to both the new investor and the more experienced. If you follow Sherman's advice in this book, you will find the means to properly manage your personal finances while adhering to scriptural principles. Rest assured that you will not find any 'name-it-and-claim-it' theology herein or alarmist forecasts; instead, the reader will be shown how to properly and wisely invest monies for a host of needs in the future. Being wise stewards is a calling all believers have; Sherman Smith effectively shows us a means to that end.

I have known Sherman Smith for approximately three years, during which time we have developed a new friendship which I have come to treasure. Sherman is an articulate and compassionate man, highly competent in his field. What the reader will find in this book are some real gems of wisdom gained over decades of experience from an expert in his field, a man not given to Chicken Little proclamations of the impending collapse of world economic systems as a result of a worldwide conspiracy.

Ah, a breath of fresh air.

Gregory S. Camp, Ph.D.
Associate Professor of History, Minot State University, Minot, ND
Author, *Selling Fear: Conspiracy Theories and End-Times Paranoia*

PREFACE

Prior to my career as an investment advisor, I was doing a lot of work counseling with families concerning problems they were having handling their finances. My whole theory is based upon the assumption that the reason Americans are financially dysfunctional is because of a generational problem. In other words, we are not properly taught in the home, school, or church about how to function financially, resulting in many generations being ill-educated about handling their finances.

Then, as now, I was active lecturing around the country as to how these problems occur and just how to go about fixing them. In fact, that is the subject of my next book, so we'll attack that problem later.

Now keep in mind that years ago, I was not trained as a financial advisor; I was a minister and was simply giving general financial advice that seemed right for my audience.

After a lecture one evening, a neatly-dressed man walked up to me and pointed out that I was giving some great advice during my seminar. He then commented that, in addition to financially dysfunctional audience members, I must also have some people attend who are financially functional in their thinking, but who get into trouble with less-than-astute choices about how to handle the money they have accumulated during their lifetime. He pointed out that this is a big problem in many American homes. Millions have no place to invest their money except the bank; they lack serious investment alternatives and the information/education to evaluate those alternatives.

He was absolutely right. Many folks had been seeking my advice as to how to invest their money. I told him that I more or less had ignored those requests because I was not in the field of investments, and therefore I had no specific financial counsel to give.

He then asked to whom do I send these people for the proper advice.

When I told him, "No one," he asked me why not.

The answer was that I really didn't know anyone in the business, and I would have a hard time sending people to someone for financial advice whom I really didn't know or trust.

He then asked, "Do you trust yourself?"

Stunned, and not knowing why he was asking all these questions, I replied, "Yes, I do trust myself."

He replied, "Then why don't you take your own advice, and get into this field to give folks accurate advice from someone you trust?"

Thus my business was born—because the gentleman I was speaking to was one of the regional owners of a brokerage firm in the San Francisco Bay Area. I believe his first intention was to seek prospects for his own business, and he quickly understood that I had a ready-made market at my fingertips.

At that time, I knew nothing about the investment business, but I was given the opportunity to be trained by Mr. John Polhemus, whom I consider a guru in the industry. John took me under his wing and personally taught me the business. Later I was privileged to work with Mr. David Clarke, who understood exactly what I was trying to do. David took on the responsibility of 'plugging me in.'

I went to work as a stockbroker for Thomson McKinnon Securities and then went on to Prudential Bache Securities. I learned the business and when people would approach me during my seminars and ask where they could find an investment advisor, I was the man! Not only could I suggest what they might do, I could actually do it for them.

Over the years I became disillusioned with the pressure that is put on brokers by their firms to sell their own proprietary products (I'll explain this later in the book) and other investments that aren't always best for their clients. I know it bothered me when this pressure was applied to me. So I decided to get away from that pressure and go independent, starting my own practice.

That business grew steadily, but as time went on, I realized that a change would someday take place in the industry, as the investing public became more aware of how stockbrokerage firms generate commissions, getting a commission on every 'buy' or 'sell' they do for their clients.

In fact, I believe that in a few years, there will be no such thing as up-front commission charges on investments, and the commission-based brokers of today will end up in another line of work. This will be a welcome relief to many investors, who have seen large chunks of their life savings go down the tubes by 'churning' and other such unethical practices (I'll explain 'churning' later). I believe that the industry is moving to alternate means of generating revenue from their clients—namely, a fee basis (vs. a commission basis) for professional investment management.

Now please understand that I am not herein advocating a mass exodus away from commission-based products, because there are still many, many qualified financial advisors and brokers that do business on a commission basis. In addition, there are lots of quality investments out there which generate their selling revenue through commissions. I'm just predicting a gradual, but sure, trend away from that way of doing business.

With this understanding, and with the opportunities opening up for me, I met Mr. George McCuen, who now is president of our company. George is a successful Certified Financial Planner (CFP). Although I am still not 'gung-ho' on the financial planning business, I greatly respect accomplished CFPs like George.

George came with a problem of his own. He was frustrated because financial planners as a rule do not run investment portfolios, do not research investments per se, and do not trade investments on a day-to-day basis. He also knew that my clients needed estate planning advice, tax advice, trust advice, etc. and that I, like most stockbrokers, didn't (and often couldn't) give it to them. He thought that we could combine talents and offer a full range of services between us.

We combined our ideas and SSS&A Investment Advisors, Inc. was born. We became the first and, at that time, only Registered Investment Advisory firm in the entire Bay Area—where the corporation, not its individuals, is the Registered Investment Advisor. We put a team of young professionals together from both the commission-based stockbrokerage world and the financial planning world. We combined our skills as researchers, brokers, and estate planners, and started managing our client portfolios on a fee basis instead of a commission basis.

Over the years through experience and my education, I developed the investment management strategies which are taught in this book. In order to make the material in this book more user-friendly, I've set it up in such a way that it reads like many of my conversations with audience members at my seminars, or conversations I have with potential clients. I use a question-and-answer format, using questions I believe my readers have on their minds. The questions are in italic type, the answers in regular type.

One of my strategic approaches, the Context-Sensitive Investment Strategy (C-SIS), is the title given to my ideas by my agent and editor, Duncan Jaenicke, after interviewing me extensively about my theory and practice of investment management. In essence, Duncan put a nifty handle—a title, a focus—on the body of knowledge, techniques, and strategies that I had developed over the many years I've spent in the investment world.

Looking back over the years I've spent in this field, I owe an inestimable debt of gratitude to a couple of top-notch investment brokers who believed in my potential during those early years as a rookie stockbroker, and who then networked me into the investment advisory business on my own. I will be forever grateful to those men—and to my clients, who have trusted me over the years to guard and grow their money. They are really responsible for whatever worth I have.

I hope that this book is a small way to give back to them, and at the same time, a way to reach out and help make the world of investments a little more understandable to my new friends, my readers.

PART 1:

A FEW PRELIMINARY MATTERS

CHAPTER 1

The Myth of the One-Size-Fits-All Investment Formula

Investing seems to be essentially easy—you just buy low and sell high. Isn't that all there is to it? Aren't we making a mountain out of a molehill to say that it is complicated and requires careful study and preparation?

Often that is what the public believes. But it's a fallacy to suggest that investing is easy. In reality, it is extremely complicated.

For example, many folks think that when others are selling their investments, they should sell theirs too. It's somewhat of a 'herd mentality.' But John Templeton, who founded some of the greatest mutual funds the world has ever seen, buys when everybody else is selling. His practice goes somewhat against the grain and opposes the buy low, sell high philosophy. However, the Templeton Foreign Fund is one of the best funds that has ever come across the marketplace. Today many financial advisors and fund managers share his 'contrarian' philosophy—that is, going against the crowd.

Isn't there a classic, or timeless, approach to investing that will work well for any environment?

To be sure, there are some enduring values to good financial management, but as far as a strategy that is changeless, I don't go for it. That's why I've developed C-SIS, the Context-Sensitive Investment Strategy, which we will explain throughout this book.

Change is inevitable—that is what I have found throughout the years I've spent in the markets.

History can teach us lessons about these changes, and in this book we'll be dealing with some important historical facts to enlighten us as to what's happening now. Someone has said that the only thing new in the world is the history you don't know. I couldn't agree more.

We seek to identify trends; we're always looking back to see if anything mirrors in the past what is happening right now. And we almost always find something that does. The person who is going to get slam-dunked (i.e., battered) in the investment world is the person who doesn't pay attention to changes in the marketplace and make adjustments accordingly.

One of the mistakes that has been made by many, many financial people is that they go out too far with their investments. (By 'out too far' I mean buying an investment that locks you into a long period of time, such as a 48-month CD [Certificate of Deposit].) Inevitably, changes come during that period of time, and thus they are locked into a vehicle that now makes no sense, given the changes that occurred. In contrast, C-SIS keeps everything on a short-term basis. That way, we can change our strategy if market conditions warrant.

For instance, if I buy an investment that pays 6% interest at a time when the going rate is only 4%, that sounds good. But if I have to tie it up for 14 years to get that rate, then I may have made a bad decision. Because interest rates may very well rise in 14 years, and I am not going to be able to take advantage of that, because I have my money out too far.

It seems like the pace of change in our society becomes faster and faster every year. Are you saying that we should take this rapid change into account and let it affect how we manage our investments?

Correct. Ironically, the only thing constant in our lives today is change. My position is that there is no set investment formula we can use. We have to flex constantly.

Shouldn't my investment portfolio be similar to everyone else's?

Well, not really—because every individual is different. Their goals are different. For instance, you have some people whose goals are to buy a new boat, a new car or a new house—they essentially want to spend their wealth, not save it or build it. Obviously their goals are going to be different from a person who says, "I want a secure income of a certain amount of money for the rest of my life." So because of individual differences, portfolios (i.e., their collection of investments) have to be structured accordingly.

One of the first things we do when we sit down with a prospective client in my business is interview him to see what that person's short- and long-term goals are. That way, the financial advisor can get a feel as to what this investor wants to accomplish in the future via his investments.

There are many factors to consider. For example, personality has a lot to do with what the advisor does.

Do you mean the personality of the advisor, or of the investor?

Both, really, but here I'm speaking of the investor's personal style. You can tell by sitting down and talking about these things, and determine if a person can take a certain amount of risk, or not. Also, you can tell if he's a person who is going to constantly want a lot of feedback from you as to what's happening with his investments, or if he is just going to leave the money in your care, take a trip around the world, and essentially say to you, "Hey, you do your best and I'll come back to get it in 20 years." The latter type of investor trusts you and doesn't want to be bothered. We get all types, and we are willing to serve them according to their personalities.

Everybody's life circumstances are different, too. If you have a person who has been in a car accident, for instance, and who cannot work for a lengthy period of time, obviously you are going to treat his investment portfolio differently than you would a guy who runs five miles every morning. Same if the investor is 25 years old, versus 75 years old. Or if they have a young family, versus being a retiree with no heirs. You customize their investment strategy accordingly. Even geographical location has a lot to do with the portfolio and how you invest it and set it up.

How would geography play a role?

Let's say that a person is living in an industrial area where virtually 100% of the jobs are tied to one sector of the industry. Say it's a steel mill town in Pennsylvania. The possibility would exist that the steel mill would go out of business and everybody in town would lose their job, which has happened all too often in our country. Same deal with the automobile industry; it can grow or contract, and people's livelihoods are affected. So the portfolio should be based upon the person's geographic location; you need to be sensitive. This would be in contrast to a doctor, say, who can take a little more risk because his practice has been thriving for 20 years, and who is working in health care—a growing field—versus steel production, which has been declining of late in the U.S.

In other words, with the steel worker you would want a more cautious structuring of their investments, whereas with the doctor you can afford to take a few more risks?

Exactly. So portfolios are never the same. It's like the situation you have with snowflakes: they're all different when you look at them closely.

Speaking of steelworkers and doctors, is the old expression, "The rich get richer, and the poor get poorer" true in the world of investments?

It can be. Unfortunately, to get the very, very best investment advisors available can be tough for the little guy. For instance, a person who has $2,500 to invest is rarely going to get the attention that a person who has $250,000 to invest does.

Attention from whom?

Attention from the person who is going to be earning commissions from the investments. It's just obvious. A lot of investment advisors have minimums—that is, they won't open a new account for less than, say, $50,000 invested. So in this sense you are segregating people who have less money to invest; they won't get the attention of the so-called 'power brokers.'

Is it absolutely impossible for 'the little guy' to get expert attention?

No, there is one way: mutual funds. That's why mutual funds and other investments of that sort were invented. When you're invested in mutual funds, you have big-time financial managers working for you. We will cover this fully in our mutual fund chapter; it's the shining exception to this rule.

Earlier you mentioned the role of change as being important to investing. How do changes in, say, the political arena affect my investments?

Politics has everything in the world to do with how your investments grow—or shrink. For instance, we can go all the way back to the New Deal and see how political changes influenced the investment scene. For instance, the New Deal brought the Social Security Administration (SSA) into existence. That put the pressure on businesses to take money out of their profits that they weren't accustomed to taking out, and pay it into Social Security for their employees. Good for the employees, but bad for business. And not all good for the employee, either, because now there was less of his paycheck available to go into savings or investments to fund his future; he was bound by law to give up part of his income to fund the SSA. And during the late '80s and early '90s there was a great deal of fear among the American people that the Social Security system was going broke because the government hadn't properly invested the money, and because Congress was always borrowing from it for other spending. Those are a couple of significant ways politics play a role.

But the biggest way politics affect investments is when the government changes the tax laws. I cannot tell you how many dozens and dozens—perhaps hundreds of times—that the tax laws have been changed. Let's take one presidential administration for example—the Carter administration. We had just come out of a recession during the Nixon administration, from '72 through '74 (the exact dates of that recession depend on what economist you are reading).

We had just come out of a recession triggered primarily by the oil crisis of the early '70s. Only three or four years later, the Carter administration came in and raises taxes. So what that did was send the banking industry into a recession. Home loans, construction loans and the building industry in general went into a recession, along with the rest of the economy. We nearly bankrupted our country in a two-year period. We had more banks go broke during that period than went under during the Great Depression, or during any other period in our history. Yes, political changes can have an enormous influence on the economy.

So do financial counselors keep up on tax laws as well as what is happening on Wall Street?

The financial counselors should keep up with the tax laws, and if they don't, they are not doing their job. For example, if somebody comes in with a portfolio of stocks, and you just sell it for the commissions you can earn, very possibly the investor is going to have a huge tax consequence if he made a big profit (known as a 'capital gain') on the sale. The financial advisor should keep that in mind as he decides what to do with the investments.

How do changes in the social environment affect the way I should invest?

Some people are very socially conscious today. For instance, I have one client who will not invest in any company which is not environmentally cautious. So I have to find companies that don't pollute the environment, or who haven't been fined by the government for polluting the environment, or don't make products that would potentially pollute. It makes investing for them very, very difficult.

Similarly, you have some religious people who do not want to buy stocks in companies that manufacture tobacco or other so-called vices. Because R. J. Reynolds grows and sells tobacco (but they do multitudes of other things as well), they won't invest in R. J. Reynolds because of the tobacco thing. The same goes with companies that sell alcohol or deal in the gambling market. They will not invest in casinos, race tracks, things like that. In fact, there is a mutual fund which strictly keeps the investors away from any of those socially-sensitive activities. So in that sense, the changes in our society do affect one's investment strategy.

Does socially-sensitive investing make sense from a business point of view?

Socially-sensitive investing makes sense, it seems to me, as long as it doesn't hurt the overall financial position of the investor. There is an element that the sales reps who are selling socially-conscious funds often overlook, or leave out: do they make money or do they lose money? That's the point. I think we are missing a big, big, point when we get caught up in 'saving the whales' and yet lose 20% of the investor's principal each year because some of these funds are dogs (poor performers).

Plus, we have a blind factor here. That is, a person who invests in a CD at the bank doesn't know what the bank is going to do with that money. The bank takes that money and loans it out to businesses and corporations—many of which are like R. J. Reynolds or Harrah's Casino. These are good money-making stocks, and banks don't miss the opportunity to invest in many of those. So it is not always possible to hold the line on this sort of thing.

However, I think that directly investing into a company—that's a different ball game entirely. There are thousands of companies that accept direct investments (we'll cover that in detail later in the book), and you don't have to buy cigarette companies' stock if you don't want to. There are certainly other stocks that perform well; you don't have to be in the gambling business to make money! But if you are going to buy a mutual fund, many of them may have a very small position at times in one of those co-called 'bad' or 'immoral' companies. I think it gets a little silly to kick a mutual fund out of one's consideration simply because the fund has some activity in these types of businesses.

How have changes in technology affected the way I should make investments?

Technology has changed the whole industry and continues to do so. A lot of people have a fear of technology; they are afraid that the government is going to get control of their money and drastically invade and control their lives. And while a few of those fears might be well-founded, at the same time we can't do business without technology because, like I said before, change is inevitable. It's just going to happen. I mean, who wants to go back to the time when you couldn't get money out of an ATM (automatic teller machine)?

Because of improved technology the average layman is becoming more acquainted with the investment world. For instance, today you can buy some investments directly from the company issuing the stock; a person can call an 800 number and do it themselves without going through a stockbroker. You can manage your own portfolio by using a discount broker.

Or you can manage your own portfolio by using software on your personal computer. Online services like America Online, CompuServe, and Prodigy give stock reports that are delayed only 20-30 minutes from actuality, and you can run your own investment portfolio from there, if you think it's a wise idea (I'll cover later on why I think that's a bad idea for most investors). Improved technology has allowed people to do that.

Another thing: technology has prevented the stock market from crashing so often, or so hard. After the Great Crash in 1929, certain laws were put into place to act as stopgaps. And that was the forerunner of what happened after 1987, when the stock market crashed again. It fell over 500 points in one day. They called it Black Monday—it was Monday, October 19, 1987. It was bigger than the 1929 Crash.

Yet, three months after the stock market crashed, there was no proven adverse effect on the U.S. economy. One of the reasons for that was that 'circuit breakers' had been put into place, which are based on technology. Though that one-day drop was precipitous and quite scary, it didn't lead to 'The Great Depression, Part II,' as some doomsayers would have us believe.

I experienced these circuit breakers myself when some years ago I wanted to sell Burger King stock. At that time, I carried a big, big position in Burger King stock in my clients' portfolios. I wanted, in one day, to make a trade of tens of thousands of shares. So we called the trading desk in New York and put in our sell order. I wanted to take a profit and invest the money in something else. But they wouldn't let me do it because they feared such a large sale would adversely affect the price of the stock—the next morning or perhaps in the next hour. It was technology, then, that prevented that from happening—a circuit breaker. So I was only allowed to sell off a few thousand shares at a time, each day. It actually took two or three months to liquidate our holdings in Burger King.

How do changes in inflation affect my investments—and how can I compensate for that effect ?

Inflation is the phenomenon where prices go up, effectively making our money worth less with each hike. For instance, if inflation is on the rise, then the prices of things we buy are going to be on the rise too.

On the other hand, if we are into a more deflated economy, like we were in the early '90s, where the prices of things were coming down—we call that 'deflation.' (There is a middle ground, where inflation is not roaring up or down, but middling along; this is called 'stagflation.')

Inflation can affect investments by, say, affecting the bond market. Although we'll cover bonds in greater detail later in the book, let me just say briefly here that there is an inverse relationship between bond prices and interest rates. As interest rates rise, bond prices come down. As interest rates fall, bond prices go up. For example, in the spring of 1994 to January 1995, we had rising interest rates. So people who had big bond holdings feared that their bond prices would fall, which is exactly what happened. Many people lost a lot of money in the bond market during that time. So inflation is extremely important.

How do I compensate for inflation? Well, there are investments we can insert into the portfolio called 'inflation/deflation hedges.' An example would be to find an investment that has a constant yield, say, of 8%. Everything in the investment world revolves around a rule of thumb of about 8%. If you get 8% most—or all—of the time, you are doing pretty well. So even if the going rate for earnings is 12%, you still are doing pretty well at 8%. If the going rate for earnings is 6% or 5%, you are doing great with 8%. So let's say you had some investments that are in there for 8% on a constant basis, not changing with the tide of inflation. Then you have an inflation/deflation hedge.

Inflation is like a balloon that is small when deflated, and then gets big when it is inflated. It is a bubble which, if not controlled, will pop. So inflation means that the prices of things are increasing ahead of the earnings arena's ability to keep up with it. The fears of some economists—I call them doomsayers—is hyper-inflation. That is when normal inflation gets out of control (e.g., above our normal range of 4-5% or less). We see this in third-world countries. I'll get into this in chapter 3, but for now suffice to say that I don't think this is a real danger for the U.S. economy in the near term. I also cover this in more detail in my first book, *Exploding the Doomsday Money Myths: Why It's Not Time to Panic.*

How do changes in the federal deficit, and/or the federal debt, affect how I should invest?

The federal debt has no effect, but the federal deficit certainly does.

Could you define both those terms—deficit and debt—for me?

The federal *deficit* is when the government is spending more money than it takes in year by year. The federal *debt* is the total money we owe on the money that we have borrowed over the years.

There is a misconception of how to interpret the dangers of the federal deficit and debt. The public usually looks at the federal deficit the same as they look at a household deficit. And they also look at the federal debt the same as the debt of private individuals—but it is an interpretation which is faulty.

The reason it doesn't hold up is because the government plays by different rules than you and I do with our creditors. The money that we (i.e., the U.S. government) owe, we owe to ourselves, in that we have largely borrowed it from American investors. Between 85-88% of the federal debt is owed to Americans in the form of treasury notes, treasury bonds, and treasury bills, held in retirement accounts and the like, contrary to some doomsayers who say that the Japanese are our biggest creditors, or the Saudis, or some other foreign group. In reality, only about 12% of our federal debt is owed to foreign investors.

So the deficit is not as dire as some people make it out to be?

Right, it's not. It is not a big bogeyman that we need to be afraid of. The federal deficit simply means that you are spending more money than you are taking in. A private household cannot operate at a deficit very long because there are dire consequences for doing that—you will eventually wash out. The federal government, in contrast, can go on and on and on.

There are two reasons the government can do that. Number one is that the government is sovereign, so it can do anything it wants, at any time it wants. A household, in contrast, is not sovereign.

Number two is that the government can raise taxes to bring more money into the treasury. Also, the government can create jobs, which bring in more taxes. So the government can continue to operate on a deficit for a very, very long time.

Plus, even with all its faults, our federal legislature has the ability to keep things in good shape through its checks and balances over time. In that sense, I'm quite different from the doomsayers, who have little faith in our governmental processes. For instance, if you look back at the congressional election of 1994, you will see that there was a backlash among the American public; they said 'enough is enough.' A huge number of Republicans got elected. They got control of Congress back after many decades of Democratic dominance.

So in early 1995, during their first 100 days, one of the main points of their agenda was to straighten out the deficit problem. And part of the way to do that was to seek to pass a balanced budget amendment to the U.S. Constitution, to directly attack the debt and deficit problem. (As of press time for this book, that amendment had not passed both houses of Congress, but came within one vote of doing so, a record for such a measure. There was momentum to revisit that issue soon thereafter. The point being, that for Congress to even bring such a radical step close to completion was a monumental task and showed its resilience in fixing economic problems faced by the country.)

How should changes in interest rates affect my investment planning?

Well, rising—or falling—interest rates will dictate how your financial advisor is going to structure your investments. For instance, if stock yields (i.e., earnings) are 5.5% and interest rates are 2% the investor is not going to buy CDs (which are based on interest rates paid by banks). He's going to invest in whatever makes more money and still be in a fairly secure position. He may go to a bond (a fairly safe investment) that is yielding 6.5%. It might be a government-guaranteed bond of some kind.

So interest rates should affect your planning all the way around. I already stated that if you have your portfolio committed too long-term and then interest rates go up, you'll get caught in a poor situation, because you can't take advantage of the rising rates. So the C-SIS method always has the financial advisor—and the investor himself—on his toes, to see what is happening today and positioning himself to take advantage of the trends.

For instance, I sold out of some of my more risky bonds prior to the interest rates being raised in the fall of 1994, to protect my investors from losing money. So I have to pay attention to the rise and fall of interest rates, or what I think the federal government is going to do in that regard. I listen to the news and pick up these little tidbits. If the Fed (the Federal Reserve Board, something I cover in more detail later in the book) is saying they might raise rates in two months, that is a signal to me that they are probably going to do that. So I may have to reposition my portfolio accordingly. But if I am in a position where I can't do that (i.e., having money locked into long-term situations), I'm stuck. Interest rates are going to directly affect the value of that portfolio. They can do that in one day, or even in one night.

Just as there are trends in interest rates, there are trends in the stock and bond markets. Right?

That is correct.

How are those trends important in planning my investments?

As I often state, the past is very, very important. We look at trends to see if anything politically or anything in the U.S. marketplace or international marketplace has occurred before that could give us insight into the future. For instance, How did the Second World War affect stock prices? If today we went into a war in Kuwait that escalated into the Persian Gulf Conflict, and that in turn escalated into a huge war (akin to WW II), how is that going to affect certain investments I might have? We can learn to predict such outcomes by studying history.

How can the individual investor either spot these trends or know what to do about them?

Well, first off, this is why most investors need a financial advisor to advise them, experts in investments. 'Going it alone' is foolish in my view.

Second, if I as a financial advisor think we are going to have a big war, I don't want to be in too many automobile stocks, because the automobile plants in World War II were changed into bullet factories and plane factories; they converted to making tanks instead of cars. As a result, we didn't have a 1942, '43, '44 or '45 automobile. We had '41s and then we had '46s. The car business declined greatly during those years, and I wouldn't want to 'lose my shirt' because of that change.

That is a rather extreme example; if you wanted to fine-tune that, you can look at other industries that have been affected by history. For instance, if you go back to the early 1900s there were people who invested in horseshoe factories. Today you can't find one horseshoe factory on the New York Stock Exchange. They don't exist. The same thing with buggy whips and every other thing related to the horse-and-buggy days. If you don't pay attention then to these trends, I will guarantee you that the same products that we are using in 30 years will not be the same products we are using today. We will have a whole new list of stocks on the stock exchange.

Therefore, the old adage about 'investing your money and then forgetting about it' may not be true in a certain sense—correct?

It has never been true; you always have to keep your wits about you in terms of the changing scene and how it can affect your investments.

That wrong thinking is what ruled people's behavior historically regarding real estate. They thought real estate was going to be a strong market forever. But then we had a big economic correction in 1992. People forgot, or didn't know, that inflation drives real estate markets. We had inflation for 70 years and then all of a sudden in 1990 we didn't have it anymore. Inflation was becoming stagflation, and then became fairly rapid deflation in terms of real estate prices—especially in California, where I live. Therefore, real estate prices fell, and stayed down for some time, until inflation returned. So during that time, if you had every single dollar of your money in real estate you suffered some big losses.

So are you saying that real estate is not a good investment?

No, I am saying that real estate might be an investment to consider, but certainly there are other investments that I would consider over and above it. For instance, the stock market has outperformed every other investment, including real estate, since 1936. Hands down.

So you are saying real estate could be an acceptable part of your strategy, but don't put all of your eggs in that particular basket?

Exactly.

If my broker changes investment strategies, or decides to buy or sell my investments, do I lose money?

If the broker changes the investment strategy you don't necessarily lose money. For instance, there are only two reasons to buy and sell from where I sit. One is either to protect your profit, or two, to limit your loss. So if you have a stock that is going down, obviously your broker has to make a decision.

What is that decision he must make?

The decision would be to sell, if he thinks that the stock is going to drop further, therefore limiting your loss. At the same time, the broker must make a decision at some point in time when you have enough profit and he wants to diversify the money into other kinds of investments, and to protect your profit he sells. Those are the only two reasons to sell investments.

But sometimes brokers make mistakes—they're human, too. He makes a bad call or he makes a mistake. That happens and is part of life in the investment world.

Some investors don't want a notification from the financial advisor for every little transaction; others do. For instance, one of our policies at my firm is that we notify every investor before we change the strategy, unless they've indicated up front that they don't want to hear about it. If we have a stock or something in the portfolio that is in jeopardy, and we can't get ahold of the investor by phone in time, we may go ahead and make the decision many times to sell that stock without the investor's prior knowledge. Such a move is in the best interest of the client, and we feel that the advantages outweigh the disadvantages.

Now some investors don't want notification in advance of our 'buy' or 'sell' moves; they tell us that in the initial client interview. Most investors will say, in effect, 'I hired you to make these decisions, just go ahead and do it. I am turning this over to you. I trust you to make the right decision.' To answer your original question, if the broker changes investment strategies, and if he doesn't make a mistake, then you are probably not going to lose money.

CHAPTER 2

The Context-Sensitive Investment Strategy:
How It Works—and Why

What exactly is the Context-Sensitive Investment Strategy?

The Context-Sensitive Investment Strategy, or C-SIS for short, describes an approach we developed several years ago because of the changes that were happening in the international markets. Back then, we paid little attention to third-world markets because there was little to no middle class in those countries. In contrast, today there is a growing middle class in the third-world markets that is soon going to be buying virtually every piece of technology Americans make.

China is the biggest of these markets, of course, with 1.5 billion people who are going to be significant consumers someday. And the former Soviet Union is going to count, too. Any of the third-world nations is now worth planning for. China is probably the biggest market I am thinking about—everything that the U.S. manufactures, sings, records, eats, and drives is going to be devoured by this emerging middle class. Thus the opening up of once-closed markets, such as we saw with Japan decades ago, has huge implications.

Today you cannot have a portfolio which does not pay attention to the world economy. And these changes are even more rampant and hard to track than those in the U.S. economy, which is changing fast, too. Under the C-SIS model we invest based upon the context of what is happening politically, socially, and economically, both nationally and internationally. C-SIS pays attention to these climates so that the investor can take advantage of the enormous amount of good solid investments all over the world. We're not limited just to our economy, if our economy is declining.

Plus, international markets offer potential for U.S. companies—and their investors—to make a lot more money than they previously had. So it's a double-win situation that benefits investors both directly (by having foreign stocks perform well) and indirectly (by having domestic stocks perform well, due to new markets opening up to them). Under C-SIS, we can take advantage of all the opportunities available.

So it sounds like one of the chief benefits of C-SIS is its flexibility and adaptability.

Yes, flexibility and adaptability are key concepts in this strategy.

Can you think of any examples where C-SIS put your investors in a good position?

Today we are developing our portfolios with a generous position in international markets. We buy both international mutual funds and some foreign currencies. We're even investing in things like Swiss annuities, which have more 'bells and whistles' than annuities do in this country.

What is unique about C-SIS?

Well, C-SIS is our philosophy, but it is not entirely unique; the best financial advisors around the world have always been adapting their strategy to fit current conditions. The term C-SIS itself is unique, which rather neatly describes what we were already doing prior to my writing this book. It essentially takes a cross section of philosophies from many different financial advisors and puts the best of all that into one cohesive strategy.

Can an average investor use the C-SIS method to run his or her own portfolio? Or does it require an expert?

Just like a surgery patient who wants to direct his own operation in the operating room of the hospital, people make a big mistake today by not having financial advisors on their team. It is almost impossible for a person to make any serious money managing his own portfolio. I know very, very few people who do it, or do it well. In fact, I don't know one single person who does it successfully. There may be some out there, but I don't know them. I'd say that if they are doing it successfully, they are not true lay people, but rather almost professional money people themselves. Look at Warren Buffett, the most successful single investor in history. He started out as a simple investor, but now he's an expert. That's inspiring, but it's not typical. So I'd say that 99.9% of folks out there should use a financial advisor.

So the do-it-yourself philosophy in the complex world of investments is largely a myth?

Exactly. It won't work because we have advisors who work all day long doing technical or fundamental analysis on which investments make sense to commit to, and which don't. Unless private investors have the expertise to sit there eight hours a day and figure out the marketplace, then they can't make C-SIS work on their own.

What I want to do in this book is educate the reader enough on this philosophy so that he can work with a financial advisor and know enough about it to gauge whether the financial advisor is doing a good job for him— or not. It has to be a teamwork thing, and this book will educate both the investor and the financial advisors out there who need to learn more about C-SIS.

What do you mean by "technical and fundamental analysis?"

Fundamental analysis basically concentrates on healthy companies; analysts evaluate the soundness of the corporation by looking at fundamental concerns, such as the economy, the political climate, or the competitiveness of the particular industry.

Technical analysis is different. It's not concerned with inflation, or the prospects of a particular industry, or whether an industry is going to increase its dividends (regular payments to stockholders) on its stock. Instead, in technical analysis they look at the numbers a particular company generates. Things like trading volumes, at what level the account opens, where it closes, etc. So they are looking at the technical statistics, rather than the overall broad picture of the marketplace.

Getting back to the do-it-yourself philosophy, what if a person is very independent and doesn't really believe that C-SIS is too complicated for the average investor? What would you say to him or her?

I would say that it would be like getting on an airplane and deciding that you wanted to fly the plane yourself, without any formal training in flight school, versus letting the professional pilot do it. It's rather foolish. When I get on an airplane as a passenger, I know things *about* the plane. I know it is an L-1011 or a 747 or whatever; I know it has wings, and I know it has wheels, and I know it takes off and lands. And I know I want to go to Boston. But I want somebody that knows exactly how to get me there, and in good shape. That is why I pay the fare and get a pilot who knows how to do all that. I trust in that pilot, rather than trying to do it on my own. I want a pilot who has flown through a storm or two.

So, really, most people do need some type of financial advisor.

Yes. It is very difficult for the average investor to make quality investment decisions without some quality advice. There is a rule that I learned when I was a stockbroker that is kind of tongue-in-cheek called 'the 90% rule.' It says that the individual investor, without the financial advisor, is wrong 90% of the time.

I agree—except in my experience, that the solo investor is wrong probably 95-99% of the time.

How can I educate my broker or other advisor on the C-SIS method?

Buy this book and give it to him or her. Better yet, buy two copies, one for yourself and one for your broker. Get the word out.

What lessons can I learn from history in terms of investing for today—and tomorrow?

One of the lessons we can learn is based on the opening of the American West. There are many doomsayers today who say that this country and its economy are going down the tubes, that the American dream is lost, that there is going to be an "economic earthquake." They write books like *Bankruptcy 1995*.

When I see such books popping up, I ask myself, *Is all this doom-and-gloom really going to happen?*

To understand whether it is or not, let's go to history. Let's go back to 1878. Did you know that we've had two depressions in this country? One was in 1878; the other was in 1929. They were both caused by different things. One, in 1929, by the manipulation of the securities and banking industries; the other, in 1878, by a totally different factor.

In the late 1800s, the American East had become saturated with manufacturing plants; they basically had tons of products with nowhere to sell them. Then the railroad opened up the entire West. So millions of pioneers poured over the Mississippi River and built towns and villages and cities all over the West. That released this pressure that was in the East because they now had a place to sell their products and expand their companies. Which is exactly what they did. That drove our economy for decades and decades—in fact, for almost an entire century.

Today we have a similar situation: we have saturated the domestic market and need overseas markets for expansion. And the doomsayers are right in the sense that this country cannot run on its own markets alone. It can't keep developing products and new technologies and inventing new things without new people to buy them. There are only so many people to consume them without other companies going broke while new companies come on the scene. If too much of that happens, the economy is going down the tubes.

What the doomsayers don't understand is history. They pay no attention to it. Today we have something happening that happened in 1878. We have markets opening worldwide. The fall of communism, which the doomsayers never planned on, has opened up a whole new segment which someday will buy American products 'big time.' Manufacturers are going to locate new plants there. This is true both in the former Communist Bloc countries and in the Pacific Rim. That latter grouping includes countries like China, Thailand, Korea, Japan, Laos, Vietnam, etc. This will drive our economy for centuries, literally.

Japan, as they get the pressure from our international trade agreement, will open up and begin to buy our products. By the way, as of mid-to-late 1994, America for the first time in history has become the number-one exporter in the world. We never were before; we always imported more than we exported. This is good news indeed.

What is the significance of that?

It is proving that I am right; that emerging markets are opening and people are buying our products. So we are now shipping our products all over the world. It is not just Americans buying refrigerators; now people from other countries are buying American products and services.

What does a typical portfolio look like when you use the C-SIS method to help formulate it?

Well, in general terms we would structure it like this:

>> 5% gold and silver
>> 5% foreign stocks
>> 5% foreign currencies
>> 55% U.S. stocks
>> 15% U.S. government and corporate bonds
>> 5% treasury bills
>> 5% foreign bonds
>> 5% cash or money market funds

Let's say that in a typical model we have 55% in stocks—we would break the stocks down into a percentage of the types of stocks we would have, like foreign stocks or stocks that pay a strong dividend, or stocks that we buy for growth. We would break it down further into particular sectors, for instance, we might have a certain percentage in manufacturing of computers, another portion in automobiles, etc.; broken down by industry.

Then we have 15% in bonds—we would break that down into different types of bonds. There are many types, which we will discuss in our chapter on bonds.

So this portfolio, then, would be sensitive to what is happening in all segments of the economy. It would be similar to what the portfolio manager of a big mutual fund would do, except that our strategy would be much more varied because we could do more types of investments than the mutual funds manager could actually do. Plus we can tailor it to that individual investor's goals and to the current investment climate.

Tell me about the Federal Reserve Board. What is it?

The Federal Reserve Board (sometimes known as 'the Fed') is a group of bankers, a private sector organization. People think that the Federal Reserve Board is part of the United States government, but it is not. It has the responsibility of controlling the money supply, and it controls inflation by regulating the money supply, interest rates, and other things.

What is the significance of knowing that it is a private, non-governmental body?

Because the government has too much control of too many things as it is; at least this is one area that the government doesn't control directly. If Congress or the government was deciding on monetary policy by themselves, that would be a very dangerous situation.

So actually we should be grateful that the Federal Reserve Board is controlling these factors, and not the government itself. Is that what you are saying?

Well, that is a controversial issue. A lot of people think that the Federal Reserve Board is composed of a bunch of conspirators, members of a secret society known as *the Illuminati,* that goes all the way back to the Rothschild family (international bankers and financiers) in Germany and a conglomerate of other organizations having to do with the Council on Foreign Relations, the Trilateral Commission, and even the Masonic Lodge—but I don't think so. That's mostly just paranoia speaking.

The truth is, we can't operate without the Federal Reserve Board. The Federal Reserve Board dictates our monetary policy. True, they occasionally make some bad decisions, but they make some good decisions too. The Fed kept us from going bankrupt after the 1987 Black Monday market crash when they made one of the most prudent economic decisions they have ever done in our country's history. They decided to pump money into the economy, and thereby increase the money supply. If they had not done that, we would have been in a true disaster following that event—perhaps bankruptcy.

What difference does the existence and function of the Federal Reserve Board make for me, as an individual investor?

The Federal Reserve Board decides what interest rates are going to be, by determining the prime rate (the interest rate it charges to its best customer banks), the federal funds rate (the rate banks charge each other for overnight loans), etc. These in turn affect things that consumers care about, like home mortgage interest rates. And all these affect investments and the economy in general.

What role does the Federal Reserve Board play in our currency—what is commonly called paper money?

This brings us to the technical term 'fiat money.' What that means is that our country now operates on currency that is not backed by a commodity, such as gold. We are not on the gold standard anymore. Contrary to popular belief, even when we were on the gold standard, only 25% of our currency was backed by gold since 1868 anyway.

In 1971 Richard Nixon took us off the gold standard and we were issued Federal Reserve Notes instead of Silver Certificates, as we had done with the commodity-backed currency. So today we operate on a sophisticated and complicated bartering system of credit, which works quite well, really. We've made it work. Those who worry about this, and yearn to return to the old system of precious metal-backed currency, are living in a dream world, in my opinion.

Tell me about this bartering system.

Say that I give you a $50 bill, a Federal Reserve Note for that amount. When I give you that note, even though the paper itself is worthless, what the government who issued it is guaranteeing you is that you are going to receive 50 dollars' worth of goods and/or services for the bill, or note, you gave me. Under the old rules, that $50 bill could be redeemed for 50 dollars' worth of precious metal, but not so today.

Though one might think that this is a shaky system, in reality it's not. Ours is one of the most robust economies in the world, and every day billions of dollars of value in goods and services change hands, without all the gold in Fort Knox backing it up. It doesn't affect our economy if that gold is nonexistent, since that's not what the system is based upon.

Put simply, it works. In a sense, it is a complicated credit system where we trade products and services to each other with the government saying that they will guarantee it all by the note we exchange. The doomsayers worry about it, but once you look at the facts, it begins to make sense, and loses any false dark implications.

It's just like in the old days before they had money—they would trade, say, 10 bushels of corn for a horse.

Right. I was on a talk show once, a national interview program with call-ins from all over the country, and one of the questions was, What is money? Well, that was a very good question.

We think of money as coins and bills. But the truth is that money is anything that works in exchange for goods and services. So if the money is a bushel of corn, then corn is money. If I give you a bushel of corn for a basketful of eggs, then we have exchanged—and that is what any economy is all about at its core.

Of particular note is that, if we had still had a currency backed by gold, then the 1987 (Black Monday) market crash would have had disastrous and long-lasting results. But since we have a more flexible system today, we were able to survive—and thrive.

Should it be a cause for concern that our money is issued by a non-governmental body—the Fed—and not by our elected government?

That's a misconception too; the Federal Reserve Board doesn't issue money. The currency is printed by the U.S. government. And the coins are minted by the U.S. government. The only thing that the Federal Reserve does is dictate the policy as to how that money is going to be used—the money supply, interest rates, etc., as we have discussed.

So even though on our paper money it says "Federal Reserve Note," that is not cause for concern because it really is the U.S. government issuing it?

Right. Again, rumors get started and are perpetuated by paranoia, largely. The facts are usually less frightening.

Tell me about another of the regularity bodies that is involved in our economy: the SEC, or Securities and Exchange Commission. What is that all about?

The Securities and Exchange Commission was created out of the Glass-Steagal Act of 1934. What this did was separate the banking industry from the securities industry so that the two markets could not be manipulated, one against the other.

The Securities and Exchange Commission today has many, many functions. Not only does it regulate the banking industry, but also it regulates the securities industry. It also regulates the stockbrokers and financial advisors in America, who are responsible to this very powerful governmental body. What that does ultimately is to protect the investor or consumer. It protects them from unscrupulous financial people who might use the investor for their own gain.

Does the SEC really have much power over financial advisors?

The SEC has an incredible amount of power over financial advisors. I don't mind telling you that they keep most financial advisors' 'feet to the fire' regarding following the laws and complicated regulations in force. Many a night's sleep has been lost worrying over what the SEC will rule or do regarding one's practice. That's bad for financial advisors, but good for the public.

One of the bodies that's part of the SEC is the NASD, the National Association of Securities Dealers, which governs the stock brokerage industry. The NASD has very, very stringent rules. In fact, ours is the most regulated industry in the world, probably. The SEC and the NASD are these governing bodies who see that 1) the broker or financial advisor is properly licensed, and 2) that he constantly keeps the rules of fair practice and ethics. When those rules are violated, then there are some severe consequences.

Such as?

The financial advisor can go to jail, for instance. He could be sentenced to jail, such as Michael Milken was in the '80s, and like many others who tried to manipulate and/or break the rules. Or he can suffer severe fines, as much as $500,000. One company, Prudential, in the early '90s had to pay $300 million in its settlement to investors for unfair practices in selling them direct partnerships. You can bet that one of these governmental regulatory agencies forced that little settlement; companies usually don't volunteer to pay out $300 million settlements!

There are severe fines levied on brokers and advisors all the time, but probably the most severe is being banished from the securities industry forever. That happens from time to time, as warranted.

These regulatory bodies even regulate *before* a person comes into the industry. If an applicant for licensing doesn't check out pretty darned clean in terms of his record, his background check, his character, etc., he doesn't get granted his license, and is effectively locked out of the industry.

I have always thought that most brokers were honest before they went into the business; they became crooks *after* the fact. They made it into the industry because their lives were clean enough that they were deemed fit for the business. They were educated and they passed the exams, they loved the business, they knew the business. But the temptation over time gets to some of them and they get involved in graft and illegal activity and then the governing body comes in and takes them out. Because without that license granted by that governmental watchdog agency, you're dead in the water.

What effect have international bankers had on the investment economy?

International bankers have really had a great effect on the economy. They inject a lot of life into our economy. Where we used to have only a few international bankers in the early part of our history, we now have hundreds of international bankers. Their function is to inject needed capital into our system to allow for expansion and growth, especially if that capital is not available from domestic sources. For instance, Andrew Carnegie, Nelson Rockefeller, Henry Ford—these great entrepreneurs of the past, whose companies still bear their names, needed capital while expanding their companies in times of great economic opportunity. Going to the local bank in their towns, however, didn't produce the large amounts they needed.

This is in the late 1800s/early 1900s, during the Industrial Revolution. There simply was not enough money available locally to finance the rapid expansion needed. So by necessity international banking was born. Money was brought in from investors around the world. And there were some very wealthy countries who wanted to participate.

Were they principally European bankers at that point in time?

Right, at that time they were mainly European bankers. Today, of course, we have Japanese bankers and other types involved. By borrowing internationally, our economy has been allowed to expand.

International bankers have been feared for eons, mainly by the type of people who thrive on conspiracy theories. These types of folks are just absolutely sure that the 'House of Morgan' (from the great entrepreneur J.P. Morgan) and other guys are part of a big conspiracy, and that the international bankers are controlling everything. Virtually everything that is sinister is somehow connected in the minds of such people with the international bankers. Things like all of the wars in history, race riots, and the list goes on. The only thing that the conspirators don't blame on the international bankers was the financing of the Genesis flood!

None of this is true. Remember when these people used to say we should fear the Japanese because they are going to buy up our nation, purchase all our real estate; that they are going to own America? Well, the truth is that right now, and in the recent past, the Japanese have made some bad deals in America and they can't wait to get out of them. In the late 1980s and the early 1990s, the Japanese sold many, many of their businesses in Orange County, California, the Los Angeles area, because of the bad investments they had made on buildings. When California's economy got in trouble—the recession of that period—the foreign investors got in trouble, too. In Hawaii today there are thousands of hotel rooms and apartments that are empty because of overbuilding; this hurts foreign landlords as well as American land owners.

But here is the big point: you can never buy a country. A country like America you must conquer. Simply buying up some real estate or some hotels or some office towers doesn't cut it. As of mid-1995, the largest foreign holder of land in the U.S. was England, and as far as I know, they didn't own us as a nation because of that!

Now a case in point is the hostage crisis of 1979-80 when President Carter was in the White House. People were saying that the Iranians had so much money from the Persian Gulf oil that they were buying up our country. For instance, somebody said one time (and I can't remember whom it was who told me) that a great portion of the state of South Carolina was owned by the Iranians.

What happened? When the Iranians took our hostages, the United States took a big chunk of their money. The United States government froze their assets and confiscated their money, and their lands, and they lost it all. It's like the old saying down in Texas: 'Don't mess with Texas.' On the international scene nobody is going to invest so much money in the United States of America as to buy the country. We have sovereignty, and they know it.

What have your experiences serving your investors taught you about the advantages of using the C-SIS method?

One reason that the C-SIS method was born is, prior to using our C-SIS strategy, we had a tendency to act like many brokers do—lock in as many yields as we can, for long terms.

Once I had an elderly couple come to me. They had a limited income based upon the limited yields they were getting off of their money in the bank. They had invested it to receive around an 8% dividend and they could get along with that fairly well.

Then the bank started lowering their interest rates. So this couple walked in one day and said, "Our interest rates are now 6% and we can no longer make a living." I knew in my hearts of hearts that this couple was going to be in even more trouble in the future. Because of my extensive research, I felt that the Fed was going to continue to lower interest rates, not raise them. So I believed that interest rates were going to continue to go down. What I didn't realize was that interest rates were going to be only 2% and 3% before long.

I told this couple that I believed that they were going to earn at least 5%—and boy, was I wrong. So I explained to them that what they would have to do in order to get their income level back up to an acceptable margin. They would have to take a little more risk. They would have to come out of the bank; I explained to them about diversification (which we'll discuss later in the book in detail). Diversification would be the key to balance the portfolio as far as safety goes and yet get their earnings as high as we could.

The strategy of C-SIS, then, directly benefited this couple because under C-SIS the investments are on a liquid basis so that if, say, CD rates go back to 8% or 9% (and that's insured by the Federal Deposit Insurance Corporation), then this couple could then go back into the bank and maintain that earnings level they wanted.

You can be sure that couple won't make the mistake they did the last time. They won't buy those jumbo CDs on long, long periods of time. They'll follow C-SIS and keep their options open.

You've mentioned how super-cautious investors can sometimes "put themselves in jail." What do you mean by that?

Well, if you are too cautious then you don't take advantage of the better investments on the market which yield more money, even though they carry some degree of risk. The more you make, the more you are going to risk. And risk and reward go together. But people become too cautious and therefore they lose money—like in the story that we just examined. They think, *I'm not at risk when I am invested in bank investment vehicles.* But you certainly are at risk in the bank. You are at *interest rate risk.*

We will talk about this type of risk, and other types or risk, in the next chapter. Contrary to popular belief, *every* investor is subject to risk of one type or another; the trick then becomes a matter of knowing what the various risks are, and matching them to your overall system of priorities.

CHAPTER 3

What About the Risk Factor?

Are most investments guaranteed?

Some are guaranteed, and some aren't.

If you're talking about the stock market or bond market, they are *not* guaranteed; there is risk involved. However, some types of investments *are* guaranteed, or insured. These would include items like a municipal bond (which is guaranteed by the government body issuing it), or a bank CD (which is backed by the FDIC [Federal Deposit Insurance Corp.] up to $100,000 of principal), or an annuity (which is guaranteed by the insurance company alone), or a Ginnie Mae bond or a t-bill (treasury bill, explained later) or treasury note (which are guaranteed by the federal government, but only to maturity). But even these types of investments, though they may be guaranteed or insured, have varying degrees of reliability in their guarantees (e.g., if the insurance company backing an annuity goes bankrupt, your guarantee is zilch; in contrast, the full faith and credit of the U.S. government stands behind the FDIC's insuring of accounts). It depends on what the investment is, as to the degree of risk it carries.

So everything has its degree of risk, whether small or large. There is no such thing as zero risk in any investment.

Tell me more about the kinds of risks that exist for the investor.

I have distilled the various types of risks into four basic types of risk.

Number one would be **market risk.** What that means is that if you are invested in, say, the stock market, you are at risk as to whether the market is going to rise and fall, and therefore affect the price of your stock on any given hour, day, or whatever. You have the benefits of the market rising, but hand in hand with that, you have the risk of it falling. You can't have one without the other if you choose to enter the stock market.

Number two would be **credit risk.** Let's take the case of buying bonds. Bonds, put simply, are promises: company X says to the investor, "Loan me $100 today and in three years we'll pay you back $130. But you cannot have your money back before the three years are up." Now of course the period of time can differ, as well as the amount of return (in this case we used 10%).

If you were to buy a bond (which we'll cover in depth in chapter 9), such as a municipal bond, or a corporate bond which pays a higher yield than average, you would be at credit risk as to the ability of that company to stay financially healthy and thus be able to pay the promised return at the time the bond matures (i.e., the end of the agreed-upon time frame). So you would be at credit risk until you actually receive back your principal (the original amount invested) and interest (earnings or return).

Number three, you can be at **interest rate risk.**

For example, you buy a CD in the bank and you have an investment insured by the FDIC, as previously explained, up to $100,000 of your principal. But remember this: no one, neither the government nor the bank, guarantees 100% of your interest. For example, if at the time of the bank's failure your principal was $98,000 and interest owing was $2,000, only the $98,000 would be insured by the FDIC—not the combined total of $100,000.

When so many banks and savings and loans (S&Ls) failed in the late '80s, many people didn't understand why their assets were frozen in the bank and why they got back less than what their accounts were worth on their statements from the bank at the time of failure. This is the reason. Savings and loans accounts are protected by a government entity similar to the FDIC, called the FSLIC, or Federal Savings and Loan Insurance Corporation. When so many S&Ls crashed, the government had to bail them out, even when the FSLIC had insufficient funds to pay investors back. That's the beauty of having the federal government guarantee accounts—it has the ability to pay back, even if it has to charge the U.S. Treasury to do it. The bailout cost us billions in tax money, but those coverages were honored.

With interest rate risk, here is what happens. Even though you are insured through your CD in the bank for repayment of principal, you are still risking what may happen to interest rates while your money is tied up there. Say your CD pays 3% and you are locked in for five years. Let's say that interest rates go to 8% during the first two years of your term. You are going to have to pay a big penalty to get out that CD (i.e., get your money back so you can reinvest it in a CD earning 8% if that's your desire). In fact, that penalty may be more than what you would have made by staying in the investment, even at the now-paltry 3%. It's a bad situation to be in, but it does happen. This is a prime example of interest rate risk.

Number four would be **inflation risk**. Inflation risk has to do with purchasing power. If, during the time period in question, inflation is high, it starts eroding your ability to purchase the goods and services you need. For example, say the price of houses goes up a huge amount, like 20% over the five-year term that you, say, have money in a bank CD. You had hoped to put this money away and then, after it had grown, to take it out and use it for a down payment on a home. But due to inflation, by the time your CD gets done growing (say, at a low 2% per year for five years, total return 10%) prices of houses are up 20%, you've lost ground to the tune of 10%. Instead of being ahead of the game, you're in the hole. Inflation has outpaced your investment's growth rate; that's what we mean by inflation risk.

So, as you can see, the risk factor is very important and a key consideration to the investor to consider when buying any type of investment, or when setting up an investment portfolio.

So does this mean that investments are only for the brave of heart and that anyone who is afraid of risk should stay out?

Part of the job of the financial advisor is to keep the portfolio on a liquid basis. This is the heart of C-SIS. Then we can adapt to the changes in the marketplace even though we can't totally eliminate every one of these risks in every case. We can at least massage the risks, manage them and control them so that the risks are not as high, so the investor is not as disadvantaged as he might be otherwise.

So back to your original question: I would say that *substantial* risks are only for the brave of heart. But *managed* risk is the kind of risk that the everyday person can handle.

The key is often whether the investor can *afford* to take a certain type of risk. A wealthy individual has more luxury in this area than, say, a retiree who has a minimal amount of money. It becomes a judgment call, and that's why financial advisors exist; they can help you make that decision, they can help you manage risk.

One of the most important things to remember about risk is that no one should ever, ever, ever invest any money unless they can afford the risk which that particular investment carries.

Are you saying that all of us are involved in some form of risk, no matter what we do, including supposedly super-secure investments at the bank?

Yes; we're all involved in risk.

When a client says to me, "I want an investment with no risk," I say, "I'm sorry, but that's impossible. Just like it is impossible to go out on the highway with your car and drive at no risk whatsoever." You take risks in every area of your life. And financial risk is just one of those.

How can I assess, or determine, my own level of risk tolerance?

I have developed a test for risk tolerance, which we use with our clients to determine their tolerance for risk-taking. As I mentioned earlier, the key factor basically has to do with the amount of 'cushion' a person has; the millionaire can gamble a bit more; the retired teacher typically cannot risk as much. There are a wide range of investments available, from the guaranteed CDs to the options market—which is the stock market's answer to the horse race. (We'll examine the options market later in the book.)

So that test would help me determine where I am in terms of risk tolerance?

Absolutely. It—or its equivalent—should be used in conjunction with meeting with a financial advisor. This is one of the primary things your financial advisor should do when he interviews you: determine your recommended degree of risk-taking. If you sit down in front of a prospective (or your current) financial advisor who doesn't ask you questions pertaining to risk-taking, then he has not properly conducted an interview, and therefore will not likely do his job as far as your investment portfolio goes. So beware.

Does the level of risk tolerance have anything to do with a person's personality— i.e., if they generally enjoy taking risks in life, or alternately, if they are very cautious, conservative individuals and shun risk in all areas of their lives?

Absolutely. Personalities have a great deal to do with a person's investment strategy, whether they are the investor or the financial advisor.

For instance, I had a client's wife come to me and said, "I need you to get control my husband's money—while we still have some left!"

I said, "What are you talking about?"

And she said, "He loves to take risks in picking the investments we make. We have lost $50,000 so far, and I'm afraid. So what I want you to do is take our money and tie it up so he cannot get at it."

So that is precisely what we did (with the husband's permission, of course), and that is where that couple's investment is to this very day. I protected their investments by buying an investment that was hard to get out of, but yet had a good enough return that the husband didn't fuss too much with me about it. Today he is very happy about that—and so too is the wife. So certainly there is a personality factor in deciding when a person wants to take risk, but you might want to counsel against it as his advisor, depending on his situation.

I always give a financial questionnaire to a prospective client before we take him on. Thus we can determine what kind of a person he is, what his assets are, and plan his portfolio accordingly. We got a questionnaire back the other day which said, "I want nothing with any risk. Keep me in t-bills and CDs." This person obviously didn't understand what we were doing in terms of risk management, so we had to sit him down for a face-to-face meeting. This person was very stoic, very straight-laced, very no-nonsense, and basically meant what he said. He really didn't care if his earnings came to only 1% after taxes; the mere thought of the loss of one dollar in principal would 'send him ballistic.' After discussing the options available to him, he still was strongly anti-risk, so we accommodated his desires. It's our job to educate; their job to choose.

In contrast to the all-safe investor, I have other investors whose accounts might drop in value (or gain) as much as $30,000 to $40,000 per day, due to market fluctuations. But they are accustomed to the ups and downs of the stock market, they're educated and experienced enough to know that if they keep their good investments in place over a period of time, their portfolio is more than likely going to make money.

What is the best level of risk tolerance to be a successful investor?

I would say a moderate risk is the most successful. I am basically a conservative person myself, so I'm not going to take anybody's money and risk it beyond any justifiable degree.

I've had people come to me and say, "Joe Broker can get me 22% earnings," and I reply, "Well, go see Joe Broker—because you're not going to get it here." Those kinds of investments are generally too risky for most folks. Now, realize that there are investments I have made that have earned far more than 22%, but they didn't do that by design. They just turned out that way; originally I planned them to make only a reasonable return. Sometimes you just get lucky.

And the opposite is true on some other investments—you plan to make a reasonable amount of money, and they up wind losing money—or making very little. But we move out of those 'losers' very quickly if we see that we are not going to earn what we expect. Diversification is the key (which we'll explain later on).

So a moderate level of risk would be the plan for most people in most cases.

It seems I could reduce my amount of risk by having a top-drawer financial advisor managing my investments. Right?

Right. This is perhaps among the most important decision you can make as you seek to maximize your financial health. Much more important than, say, deciding that now is the time to buy IBM stock. Finding the right professional to act as your advisor is critical.

What guidelines can I use in choosing a financial advisor? And, how can I be sure that he knows his business?

This is a good question because a lot of people are unaware of our industry—the public is really just becoming more conscious of the financial advisory and stockbrokerage business and the potential benefits.

So my advice would be, first of all, to stay with a full-service person who has access to the wide range of financial services and products that will benefit the investor. The first question I would ask would be, "Are you a full-service broker?" Full service means are you properly licensed to be able to sell all types of financial products, not just, say, insurance.

Next, you should ask, "Are you registered with the NASD (National Association of Securities Dealers)?" This will tell you that they have studied and taken an exam, which they passed; in short, that they have credentials.

Next, ask, "Are you registered with the SIPC (Securities Investment Protection Corporation)?" That is the agency which insures the dealer and his clients—it's sort of a counterpart to the FSLIC or the FDIC in banking situations. It's a form of insurance company for the client. So that will assure the person that they are dealing with a registered depository—a place that actually can do the investments, not just talk about them.

Next I would ask for the manager of the office. I would tell the manager, "I want a broker with some experience. I don't want you to give me a rookie with no experience." This protects the person from what are normal beginner's mistakes—they happen, but you don't want them to happen on *your* account!

Then ask for, and check, your broker's references. Ask for a couple names of some bona fide clients. True, he's only going to give you his best clients, but that's okay. Call them; it gives you something to measure by. Ask what kind of job he's done, if he's understandable in terms of explaining various investments, etc.

The next thing to do is check with the NASD and ask for a copy of the U-4 form. The U-4 is the investigative form that is updated periodically and contains information about the broker, as to whether there have been any complaints made about him to the regulatory body; if he has any legal problems, and the like.

It's like checking with the Better Business Bureau?

Exactly. Then you're beginning to accumulate enough information to make a decision about whether to hire this financial advisor to work for you.

Also ask about the person's education and professional experience. How many years he has been in this business? What field was he in before he became a financial advisor? Things like that.

What kind of things should the person look for in an educational background for the financial advisor?

Well, I wouldn't want my financial advisor with only, say, an eighth-grade education!

He should have a college degree?

In our offices we require not only a bachelor's degree, but one in the areas of finance, business, or economics. That's not true in all offices, and it's not a hard-and-fast requirement; there are some financial whizzes out there who really know their stuff and were art majors in college. But those are rare. If he doesn't have such a degree, he should have other factors that outweigh that lack.

What is the difference between a financial advisor and a stockbroker?

A financial advisor is a person who operates on a fee basis, versus the stockbroker, who operates on a commission basis—that is the major difference. The stockbroker makes his money through sales commissions based on *transactions* (whether buying *or* selling for his client—typically 2-3%), whereas the financial advisor makes his money on the *total value of the portfolio* that he is managing for the client (typically 2-2.5%). We'll cover the pros and cons of each approach elsewhere in the book, but for now, that's the chief difference.

Of the two basic types of financial advisors—commission-based on one side, and fee-based on the other—which is the better kind?

I got my start in the financial industry as a stockbroker, and there are some good ones out there. For some clients they make sense as the financial counselor of choice. But overall, I more commonly recommend a financial advisor versus simply a stockbroker, as the wisest partner and advisor for most investors. We have a whole section in this book explaining fee-based management, which is now the cutting edge of the financial services business.

This is a big change in the industry. I believe that, as investors become more commission-conscious and less tolerant toward getting charged a commission each time they buy or sell, in a few years we are going to see a wide-ranging gravitation toward totally fee-based arrangements.

What is the negative side of the commission-based setup?

Well, the negative side is that since the broker makes his money on sales commissions, naturally he is going to tend to generate as many commissions as possible. Sometimes that goes overboard and gets out of hand.

How common is that?

Well, even one case is too common! This practice, called 'churning,' involves buying and selling when it's not really called for to make money for the client, or when it's only marginally necessary. It's hard to detect this unethical practice for the non-expert (i.e., the investor), and it eats up earnings that should be left there for the client. Although it is prohibited in the industry, a lot of it goes on by too many brokers. By churning his accounts, a stockbroker can operate with a smaller clientele because he 'turns the money over' (i.e., buys and sells assets) more than the typical financial advisor does.

So, then, with the fee-based advisor, there is no incentive to do churning. Correct?

Right, since under his earnings arrangement it doesn't matter how many times he buys and sells investments; it only matters that he makes money for the client—and not lose any money, either, since his percentage-based fee would decline if he did.

He buys and sells on the market for a very small transaction fee, charged to him by other financial institutions, which he is going to take into consideration. His incentive is to grow the client's account as much as possible. So if buying and selling securities regularly in the account is going to reach that goal, then 'more power to him' because the more assets he has under management, the more money he makes. With a fee-based person managing your money, if the client makes money, the financial advisor makes money. Therefore, it's a win-win situation, because as the earnings increase, the investor benefits, and the advisor benefits too.

But it's not all roses under a fee-based advisor arrangement; the downside is that the financial advisor may not know what he is doing in a particular situation.

How so?

The client can be ripped off with a fee-based advisor the same as he can with a commission-based broker. That's why it's so important to choose your advisor wisely.

If the financial advisor is incompetent, the portfolio may shrink by a certain dollar amount, but his personal paycheck (that annual percentage based on the portfolio's size) shrinks by much less in terms of dollars. For example, if the portfolio lost $10,000 this year over last, the investor has lost that much. But the financial advisor has only lost, say, 2% of that amount, or 200 bucks. That's not a bad loss, especially compared to what the client lost!

The bottom-line lesson for the investor is, no matter what your arrangement with your financial advisor, you need to be diligent and informed, and make sure that you and your financial advisor are using the principles of C-SIS to build your wealth safely and steadily.

If a person is using a commission-based broker, how would they even know that churning was going on? What would be a tip-off?

In one sense, all they have to do is read their mail. First of all, they will get what we call 'confirms,' written notifications sent out to the client, on a trade-by-trade basis. They may have several of those come in the mail within three to four days. If they see an excessive amount of those, that means something is going on in the account—though whether it's good or bad remains to be seen.

Second, when they get their statement at the end of the month, that will tell them the activity too. If they're paying attention, they'll have already called their broker, or right then at the end of the month after viewing their statement, they'll call him to discuss their account. Again, let me underline that simply buying and selling investments do not necessarily indicate churning in one's account—these transactions may have been required if the value of the investments indicated it was time to sell or buy. But the point is that the broker should be able to explain why he bought or sold, in every case. If he can't, or if the explanations sound fishy or vague, 'something might be rotten in Denmark.'

In a column somewhere on the monthly statement, it will show commissions paid to date. If those are excessive, this means something might be going on in the account—something that ought to be checked. That would run up a caution flag to the investor, who should then make a call to the broker and, ultimately, if not satisfied with the broker's explanations, to the manager of the brokerage house.

How can I avoid paying excessive commissions? Are no-load mutual funds a good idea?

We will cover no-load mutual funds later on, in chapter 8, but for now, suffice to say that no-load mutual funds are a good idea, just like sales charge-loaded funds. Almost all registered financial advisors mainly use no-load funds because they don't have to pay a commission. However, there are other charges involved with no-loads—there's no free lunch, as the saying goes.

And I must point out that there are very good mutual funds which charge commissions, which perform very, very well—just as there are good performing funds that are no-loads. There are good *and* bad apples in the investment world, just like in other industries.

It depends on the individual circumstance as to whether I buy no-loads or regularly-loaded mutual funds; neither one is better than the other by virtue of the sales charges they carry—or don't carry. Beware of so-called experts who throw too many rocks at sales-loaded funds; sometimes they can be the funds of choice.

How can I determine the risk factor of various kinds of investments?

For instance, if you have a treasury note or a CD, these are fairly low risk, since they are guaranteed. On the other end of the risk scale, you have investments like oil and gas leasing.

In oil and gas leasing, you're investing in operations that are highly speculative, which literally involve drilling holes in the earth to see what kinds of liquids come squirting out. It might be oil—and you win; it might be water or mud—and you lose. The 'leasing' part of the title indicates that the operation leases the property to drill on it, retaining the rights to anything found under that land. There are thousands of holes all over America which yielded nothing but water. They have scientists who predict where to drill, but it's not an exact science by any means. It's risky and it's expensive—that's why these operations seek financial partners—to share the risk and to protect themselves somewhat.

Certainly oil and gas leasing is not going to be on the same risk level as putting one's money into a CD at the bank where you know it is going to stay safe (at least in terms of the first $100,000 of principal) and most probably grow some. Of course, the trade-off is that you can get very wealthy very quickly in oil and gas; that is not true in a bank CD.

I've heard that diversification can help me minimize my risk. True? If so, how can I diversify my portfolio?

There is a lot of misunderstanding out there about what diversification really is. For instance, I one had a client come to me and say, "I am very diversified." This was during the initial client interview.

I asked, "Where are your investments currently placed?"

He replied, "Well, I have CDs in *four* different banks." He was serious; he thought he was diversified!

That is not diversification. Diversification means placing different types of investments in different sectors of business and investing in different kinds of securities, so that if a certain segment falls in value, your entire portfolio doesn't suffer. It's akin to the old saying, "Don't put all your eggs in one basket." You want to balance out your investments, to add safety and minimize risk.

And balance is the key. For example, you shouldn't have 65% of your portfolio in investments that carry a high degree of risk and only 25% in investments which don't. Conversely, you don't want 65% of your portfolio in investments that are dogs (i.e., aren't growing and earning you money, or equity).

You evaluate your portfolio for diversification sector by sector with the C-SIS method. On the C-SIS statement, we give the investor his average yield over a period of time, say three or six months, sector by sector.

Thus he can see his diversification.

What do you mean by 'sector?'

By 'sector,' I mean a type of investment, or an area or class of investment. For instance, bonds are a different sector from stocks; currency futures are a different sector from real estate.

Let's look at an example of a portfolio that was not diversified properly before we got to it. I had an elderly lady who came to me and said she feared she was losing money on her investments. And keep in mind, this was her entire retirement 'nest egg' in one type of investment, only one sector. After looking at her portfolio, I discovered that she was in a mutual fund which had a sales commission of 8.5%! She had bought it from an insurance agent who sold those types of mutual funds, which were very popular at that time. And of course he offered her no portfolio management, no diversification—nothing—just buy the fund and hope for the best.

So what we had was a nice little old lady, 84 years old, who believed this guy in her church and put all of her retirement money into this fund. It wasn't a bad investment on its own—it even performed pretty well, prior to Black Monday in 1987. But after the crash on that day, because there was no management of this woman's portfolio, no diversification, etc., things deteriorated rapidly and no one brought it to her attention. Since her fund had been doing so well prior to the crash, she didn't bother with following it. So she got hit in the 1987 crash and lost almost 40% of her entire retirement account—her life savings. It was tragic, and it's just one story. But it is repeated far too often in millions of cases around the country.

The problem was, she didn't have a financial manager. She bought the funds from an insurance agent, so she got her statements directly from the mutual fund, which only told her how many shares she had—and didn't tell her how many dollars' worth those were. So when the fund started falling, no one called her and said, "Your fund is falling, we need to get you out of it and get into something else." Why should the fund call her when their share prices dipped? They were hoping for the best, that the shares would rebound. They are not interested in having folks get out of their own fund!

I was able to take what money she had left (thankfully, even losing 40% didn't impoverish her) and properly diversify the portfolio with the right types of investments. She has been doing very well since that particular time. But just because someone says they are a 'born-again investment person' doesn't mean they know what they are doing in terms of investments, or that you should entrust your future to them. The religious status of an individual has nothing to do with their knowledge in the investment world.

So are you saying to steer clear of Christian financial advisors?

Hardly!

No, I am staying steer clear of any individual, whether Christian or non-Christian, who tries to use religion as a primary basis for your investment business.

Certainly I am a Christian, and I believe that is *part of* the reason they should do business with me. But I want my clients to trust me with their money *primarily* because I am a good investment advisor, not just because I am a Christian. I want my record to speak for itself, not simply my religious beliefs. One's faith should be a secondary consideration in selecting a financial advisor—make sure he 'knows his stuff' and is honest first of all.

What kind of goals would you set for my investments under the C-SIS method?

There are five factors when we are building a C-SIS portfolio that we must balance against each other in order to make the portfolio successful.

Number one is **safety**. We want the portfolio to be relatively safe and with a moderate risk factor. As previously discussed, we match the degree of risk with various client factors.

Number two is **yield**. We are definitely concerned about yield (earnings) and so there is going to be a certain portion of that portfolio set up specifically for the income that it produces. That might be in either some higher dividend-yielding stocks, or some good dividend-producing bonds. Or, if using cash makes any sense, we'll suggest a CD or a money market fund.

How does cash make a yield?

Well, money market funds pay a dividend, and CDs pay interest. So when CDs make sense (i.e., they are paying 7% or beyond), we put a substantial position in cash to balance out the portfolio.

What are the other three goals?

Number three is **growth**. This part of our portfolio is not going to yield a dividend, or regular earnings. What it is going to do is reinvest itself—that is, take whatever earnings it develops and instead of going into the pocket of the investor right away, it'll be used to buy more shares of, say, a mutual fund. Then eventually the investor will benefit, due to that growth.

Then fourth is **liquidity**. We want the entire portfolio to be accessible—what we call *liquid,* not tied up—to the investor at all times. Under C-SIS there are very few long-term non-liquid portions of the portfolio.

Is C-SIS somewhat revolutionary in that sense—that there are very few long-term tie-ups of an investor's funds?

Yes, it is revolutionary in that it is a different philosophy from most. We keep things on strictly a medium-term basis, always able to be adapted to current conditions.

How about that fifth goal?

Fifth is planning for what we call 'eventualities'—that is, unforeseen circumstances or developments in the economy. We try to structure our portfolios against something that might happen economically down the road. It's hard to have a crystal ball, but we do our best to be ready for whatever might appear. This is the solid rock foundation of the whole portfolio. When we buy and sell, we are structuring and allocating assets according to eventualities. There are many type of eventualities we plan for.

For example, we might seek to protect the investor against inflation and its souped-up cousin, hyper-inflation. Many of the doomsayers (doom-and-gloom economists and authors especially) think there is a risk of hyper-inflation today. We don't give any credence to that whatsoever.

What is hyper-inflation?

Hyper-inflation inflation is when a country loses confidence in its currency, and you see inflation rates of, say, 100-2,000%—like we see occasionally in Latin American countries. The doomsayers often cite Argentina and Chile as examples, or Brazil, which is traditionally a hyper-inflation economy.

But there are many crucial differences in the economies of those countries and in the economy of the United States. That's where the doom-and-gloom authors' analogy breaks down. Without going into the whole argument here, I might point out that Argentina and Chile got their currencies under control and stabilized their economy, as did Mexico. That's not to say that things are perfect there today; things are still messy south of the border.

But here is what's important: hyper-inflation is not a concern to us (at least not in the mid-1990s, when I wrote this book). However, inflation is. We know that the Fed controls inflation by raising and lowering the interest rates. So that is going to affect our investments at all times. And we can't relax for two to three years; if the economy heats up, inflation becomes a threat. If the economy is shrinking, the Fed lets the interest rates go down, to stimulate the economy. The Fed uses interest rates as a control over the growth of the economy.

If they raise interest rates and we're locked in to 2% on CDs we bought, we lose, since we can't get those new higher rates until the CDs mature. If interest rates are going down and we have locked-in higher rates on CDs, we win. So what we try to do is position the portfolio so that it could be changed almost on a moment's notice to offset these indicators that might be tipping us off as to a change in the economy.

We use Dr. Mary Williams, who teaches at the Wharton School of Economics, and who collaborates with me on occasion, for input and advice on these matters. Dr. Williams is also involved in the Snyder Entrepreneurial Research Center, which feeds us government statistics on the economy and indicators that will let us know that some change is being made.

Also on our eventualities list is the opposite of inflation: deflation. We know that if the economy is deflating, or contracting, with prices also falling, then a period of growth is surely going to come next. Growth always comes after a period of shrinkage; the economy is cyclical—up and down, up and down. So we may want to buy into a sector of the economy like, say, automobiles. Here we're betting that the price of automobiles might stabilize or come down a little bit, instead of rising like when inflation is present.

A lot of money was made in the early 1990s by our investors

through our purchasing stock in Ford Motor Company and in Chrysler.

So if car prices either stabilize or come down, that would increase sales, therefore grow the company and make your investment pay off? Is that the idea?

Yes. With increased sales come increased profits, which usually means a profit in our stock that we bought. So if a person held, say, a General Motors stock, they might get a nice dividend payment that year.

Another eventuality we plan for is prosperity. There are a couple of slang terms that Wall Street has developed which apply to this discussion: a 'bull market' and a 'bear market.' If it is a bull market, the economy is doing great. It's growing and stock prices are rising. If it is a bear market, the economy is going south: it's contracting and stock prices are falling.

So in the case of pending prosperity, if we believe that we are going to go into a strong growth period, we might want to reposition our portfolio, taking a bigger position in stocks for designed for growth, rather than yield. By this I mean we are predicting that these companies are going to have profits and that their stock price will rise ('growth'), and we will benefit by that when we sell those shares.

The last eventuality is something we don't like to talk about, but it is always a possibility: a depression. And though I am not a doomsayer by any means, and I am very 'bullish on America' and on her economy, I know that certain things *could* happen in the economy that would cause a depression. Because of that, we want a certain portion of our portfolio to be protected in case that happened. So we have a small position in gold and silver, or other such commodities that don't have any great growth, but they have good intrinsic value. In other words, even in a depression, people value gold; it's a good place to be if that ever happens. Such investments as gold and silver are the only type of investments where they can be split into a hundred different parts and each part is worth exactly that percentage of what its whole is. So this is the benefit of maybe having some gold or silver in the portfolio.

Now the term 'depression' calls forth the question of 'recession.' How is recession related to your eventualities plan?

Every seven or eight years we are going to have a recession, and so all of these things will play into the economy all of the time. The facts are that we are always either 1) heading *toward* a recession, 2) *in* a recession, or 3) heading *out* of a recession. Every seven to eight years we are going to have one; that's inevitable because an economy of this kind—a free market economy, a capitalistic economy—has upturns and downturns. Downturns are inevitable. You can't have upturns without downturns; it's just impossible—we've learned that from history.

So a C-SIS portfolio is positioned with the realistic admission that, since we're always involved in some type of recession—either in the valley heading up, or on the peak, or heading down—we'd better just deal with it. If the recession is lingering on for longer than it normally does, we had better position ourselves in the valley to be able to climb the hill and get over the top when it is time to come out.

PART 2:

HOW TO FIND THE RIGHT FINANCIAL ADVISOR FOR YOU

CHAPTER 4

Working with a Stockbroker or Other Financial Advisor

Do I really need a financial advisor/stockbroker, or can I manage my investments myself?

     Today's new computer technology allows you to subscribe to online services that have access to the stock trade, mutual fund quotes, etc. Certainly the investor *can* manage his own portfolio, and there are people who do. The question is, *should* you do it yourself?

     Managing your own portfolio is a very risky proposition if you don't know what you're doing. For instance, an investor once told me, "I can do just as well as any broker by throwing darts at the newspaper stock market quotes page and picking whatever stock the dart hits." That might have some validity on occasion, but over the long haul that is erroneous because picking stocks is a very complicated process. As we've seen from the process of technical and fundamental analysis right on through to portfolio management, there is a lot that goes into it. Just like having CDs in four different banks is not diversification, so also having a whole portfolio consisting of nothing but stocks is not wise, safe, or profitable.

So you can go to a discount broker if you don't want to pay a commission, if you don't want to pay somebody to do portfolio management for you. But it is really a pretty good deal, financially speaking, to have a broker or other financial advisor who will manage your portfolio, watch your assets, and buy and sell for you at a 1-3% charge. At the discount brokerage you are going to save a little bit of commission but you are not going to get the hands-on service that you will get from a full-service broker or financial advisor.

I like to put it this way: managing your own portfolio is like playing Russian roulette with five (out of a revolver's six) chambers loaded. Sooner or later, it is going to get you—and it'll probably be sooner! It is difficult enough in today's complex world to keep your finances healthy without having the additional stress of the do-it-yourself philosophy.

So you are saying that the small additional expense of paying a financial advisor his commission, or fee, is worth it, in terms of overall security and possible increased earnings that you receive?

Correct, just like any other profession—you get what you pay for. In legal affairs, you can go to court and try your own case, but how will you fare? Isn't hiring an attorney usually worth the expense? In 1995 a guy who was accused of shooting a bunch of people in a New York subway acted as his own attorney. He was convicted. It is much easier—and usually much safer—to pay an attorney.

So it is with your taxes. You *can* do your own taxes but because of the complex tax laws, it makes sense to hire somebody who keeps up with the latest information in this area. The same thing applies in the investment world.

To give you an example, I have had several clients over the years who gave up on the do-it-yourself model and were glad they came to their senses. I can think of one client in particular—he called me one day to discuss his portfolio. It turned out that he had his IRA (Individual Retirement Account) accounts and his other investments in two or three different brokerage houses, and he was calling all the shots—i.e., he was telling the brokers what to buy and sell in his portfolio.

What happened to him was that there developed some negative reports on some of the companies whose stocks he owned, and they all happened within a couple of days of each other. He happened to be out of the country at the particular time, and the stockbrokers who worked his account were under strict instructions that they absolutely could not make a decision without first calling the client to okay a buy or a sell. Obviously, with the negative news circulating, his stocks were falling in price pretty fast, and the standard wisdom would have been to sell the stocks to limit his loss. Action had to be taken fast to do this, but since he was out of the country, and therefore unreachable, he came back to a portfolio that lost about 35% because he wasn't available to okay the decisions. It was a comedy of errors, really. The stocks in that sector—I think it was transportation—suffered a domino effect so every one of his stocks in that particular sector got hit.

What could the stockbrokers have done if they had had a little bit of authority from him?

If they had some authority, some leeway, where he had given them some limited discretion, they would have gone ahead and protected him from losses and sold as early as they could, as the prices headed down. But when you are with a discount broker, nobody is monitoring your portfolio, so you're on your own. For every one person who is successful with the do-it-yourself approach, I could probably give you 100 who are not.

Can anybody get a stockbroker or financial advisor to work for him, or is that just for the super-rich?

The common belief among most people in America is that you have to be super-rich in order to get the attention of a stockbroker. It's simply not true. This misperception has arisen because most people don't understand what stockbrokers do.

For example, many times I will go to do one of my seminars and there are, say, 500-2,000 people there. Many times I ask the audience, "How many of you know a stockbroker personally, or deal with a financial advisor?" It depends on what section of the country I'm in, but sometimes *no one* raises his hand! I am the only financial advisor they've ever met. It's not like other professions, like real estate; almost everyone knows someone who's a realtor!

Plus there is a certain paranoia about stockbrokers, because of the negative views that presented in the media. They only hear about the bad guys, like Michael Milken, who went to prison for insider trading. The newspapers only print the scandals, and therefore the good guys are left in the dark. And there are many, many more good guys than there ever will be bad guys in our profession.

I can relate to this because when I was a boy, I used to go downtown in our city. The brokerage house had these itty-bitty narrow slat blinds, and I would try to peer in there as a little guy. It was dark in there and real scary, and I remember tiptoeing past that place when a big limousine would pull up, and out of that dark and secretive interior some big rich woman would get out, with a mink coat on, and a long cigarette, and go into the broker- age. What it did for me as a kid was connote the brokerage business as an elite profession, somewhat hands-off to regular people like me. Unfortunately, that was the way the public viewed such things back then.

Today is different; today the industry has positioned itself where ordinary people with ordinary incomes can have access to a stockbroker or financial advisor. Even though some brokers do have minimums, if you look around a little, you can still find a financial advisor who wants to help you.

What do you mean by 'a minimum?'

Big-time brokers often set minimum requirements that state, for example, 'You must invest at least $50,000 with me to open an account.' But there are plenty of brokers who will serve the little guy—often their minimums are $1,000 to $2,500.

What are stockbrokers and financial advisors like, anyway? What kind of peo- ple are they?

It takes a combination of several things to be a good stockbroker— that is why there are so few of them today. For instance, prior to 1987 there were around 88,000 full-service stockbrokers in the nation. Then after the Black Monday market crash in 1987, the industry went down to about 62,000-65,000, which was the lowest number since 1929, the year of the Great Crash.

I often compare profession against profession, like attorneys against stockbrokers, to better understand the situation. In the Bay Area of California where I live, there are 70,000 attorneys among 9.3 million peo- ple. Compare that to fewer than 65,000 stockbrokers to service the entire nation following Black Monday!

The reason there are so few stockbrokers is that it takes a combination of several things to succeed in this profession. Although attorneys are intelligent professionals, the reason there are so many of them is that Americans are litigation-happy. You can file suit over anything, and it takes a lot of the lawyers to service such a nation.

The brokerage business is somewhat of an elite business for several reasons. Number one, it takes a specialized education. You have to pass exams which are very, very rigorous. You need to study a lot after college to get qualified.

Number two, it takes intelligence, because obviously the exams are very, very hard. They are stringent, and they get harder all the time. I have new brokers telling me that the exams today are practically man-killers. They were hard enough when I took them years ago, but they are even harder today. It takes intelligence and determination to make the grade.

Number three, a financial advisor needs to be a people person. In other words, this person can't have an accountant's personality, where all he wants to do is crunch numbers. Now at the risk of offending all the accountants in the world, I must stress that the financial advisor has to be a 'people person' because he must have the personality of a professional salesman and an economist combined. The salesman in him is necessary to deal with the personalities of the clients. There is a lot of client contact in this business, and if you don't enjoy people, you'll burn out.

Number four, he must have an entrepreneurial spirit. He must have the overall focus, not tunnel vision, but the wider view of where everything is headed economically. He must be in touch with what the client wants to do as far as making the client money. Good stockbrokers and financial advisors project themselves into the client's situation so they get a feel for where the client is going, as if it were themselves. I often say, when I am interviewing a client, that I will manage the portfolio as if it were my own—or if it were for my grandmother. I am not going to take a risk for another person that I would not take myself.

It's like riding in a car with somebody else driving. That person is not going to take the risk with your life that he is not going to take with his own life. You're both in the car together. It's the same with the relationship between client and financial advisor.

Number five is that the financial advisor should have no fear of job insecurity. This person is focused; he knows where he is headed personally. Has his own goals defined and doesn't use or abuse his client to get there. For instance, I am happy when my clients are making money. I am sad when they are not. And I view myself as not doing a good job if my clients' portfolios are down in value. So we work very diligently, as any good brokerage house or firm would do, to ensure that the proper service is given to those accounts, so they perform up to par.

What are the various kinds, or types, of financial advisors available to me?

Well, there are several kinds of advisors.

On the brokerage side, you have your stockbrokers who are Series 7-licensed; this makes it legal for them to handle virtually every kind of registered investment, from limited partnerships through stocks and bonds, the whole gamut of possibilities. These brokers, as I've pointed out, charge a sales commission for each transaction. Generally they don't manage portfolios per se. They buy and sell stocks and bonds and give limited advice to their clients. But basically their job is to buy and sell. And there are many high-powered and very good stockbrokers in the industry.

Then on the other side, you have the fee-based advisors. Registered Investment Advisors (RIAs) normally charge a fee for the advice they give and/or a fixed fee on the money they manage for their clients. In some rare cases, the RIA firm may charge only for their advice and leave it up to the investor to find a broker to buy and sell investments. Unfortunately in that model, the client gets double-charged, once by the RIA and once by the stockbroker.

Do your clients get double-charged?

No. In our case, we have a registered investment *firm*. Instead of having a firm made up of RIAs (i.e., *persons* who are registered investment advisors), our *firm itself* is registered. We actually take the responsibility to both advise and do the trades, plus track those transactions in portfolio management for the client.

What difference does that make for the investor?

The RIA firm offers one-stop shopping. The client/investor can come in and not only get his estate planning done, he can also get his insurance, his stocks, his bonds and the like. Plus—and this is perhaps the most important factor of all—he gets portfolio management. Everything is taken care of. Virtually everyone who works in the firm is familiar with every single account, so the service level to the client is enormous.

Are there other types of financial advisors available?

Yes, many people go to what are called CFPs, or Certified Financial Planners. There are a ton of CFPs out there—29,655 of them, to be exact, as of January 31, 1995. CFPs generally don't want the responsibility of actually doing stock trades and keeping up with the access required to do that. A Certified Financial Planner may charge a fee to develop a financial plan for his clients. A well-designed financial plan will address five key areas for an individual: retirement, investment, insurance, tax- and estate-planning. Typically a comprehensive financial plan will cost from $1,000 to $3,000 for most individuals and should save you at least the cost of the plan in tax reduction strategies, better investment returns, reduced insurance costs, etc. A financial plan's greatest value, however, is in the peace of mind it creates by knowing where you are, where you want to go, and how to get there. It's a financial road map.

Getting back to the service that a stockbroker provides, is it true that, generally speaking, they don't provide portfolio management service, but rather just do the trades and that's it?

That is correct. The brokerage firms such as Merrill Lynch, Dean Witter, Smith Barney, and the rest, don't want their individual brokers doing any kind of planning for the individual. However, a good broker will not ignore the overall strategy of the individual investor; he would occasionally give his opinion as to where the investor ought to go in terms of strategy. But it's not his central responsibility in terms of his job description. That's why the RIA makes so much more sense for most investors.

Tell me about what insurance agents could do for an investor.

There is a series of licensure called Series 6 now, which is a limited license which allows insurance agents to sell mutual funds and variable annuities only. Many of the insurance agents now have a Series 6 license because so many mutual funds are held by insurance companies. Thus the insurance agent can directly sell mutual funds that have an arrangement with their company. So you have insurance agents out there selling mutual funds like crazy. But, in my opinion, that is a very dangerous position to put yourself in as an investor.

With all due respect to the hardworking insurance people out there, when an insurance agent portrays himself as a type of investment advisor, something is wrong. In my opinion, most agents are normally not qualified to handle the difficult world of investments with just a Series 6 license. It is really not their job. Insurance people ought to stick to selling insurance, and leave the investment advice up to the professionals in this area. It's like the old Greyhound bus commercial said, "...and leave the driving to us."

Here is another thing to note: almost all stockbrokers and financial advisors are also insurance-licensed. So if insurance was the best investment, then brokers and financial advisors would do nothing but sell insurance. Why? Because you get more commission money with insurance; it is more lucrative than individual stocks and bonds. If that was the only way to go, virtually all of us would be selling insurance! But we know better than that. Even though we are insurance brokers, we don't sell insurance unless it makes sense for our clients.

For instance, under C-SIS I have suspended buying all types of annuities that I cannot control in a portfolio. I have sold a ton of annuities in the past. I don't like the way that my annuities are performing. Because of their tax-deferred status, they might make some sense in some cases, but because of the penalties and their lack of liquidity, we're going very, very slow on them. I'll cover annuities in chapter 10.

Should I use my CPA, or other tax consultant, for my financial advisor?

Almost all CPAs have clients who want to know where to go for further financial advice. Naturally, the CPA doesn't want to rely on people he doesn't know and doesn't trust. Many CPAs don't recommend anybody for financial advice, due to this built-in cautiousness and concern for their clients. But they would like to recommend some good people if they knew and trusted them.

A big referral base for my business is from CPAs. We recently opened an office back East in which a CPA (Certified Public Accountant) has a client base which needs our services. We have had CPAs who have contacted us and said, "We don't want to manage portfolios, but we want to be involved somehow in helping our clients with their financial planning."

But my feeling is this: CPAs ought to stick to their tax advice which is, of course, vital and necessary—especially in estate planning. And we rely heavily on CPAs in our estate planning. But in general, they ought to stick to tax advice and not cross over into our industry.

Should I use the folks at my bank, who want to talk with me about investments, as my advisors?

Banks are racing into the securities business, selling things like mutual funds and annuities. This is a very bad trend, in my opinion. Though this activity is technically legal, they are stretching the spirit of important laws, such as the Glass-Steagal Act of 1934, which was put in place after the Great Depression to separate the banking and securities industries.

The reason for this activity on the part of banks is, since interest rates started dropping during the late '80s and early '90s, people fled from the banks and started going to alternate sources, like mutual funds, to get a higher yield. My business grew in leaps and bounds during those years, because of that flight from savings accounts and bank CDs. What might have been very tough for the banks was indeed a boom for my particular business.

To prevent money from going out of their business and into businesses like mine, the banks jumped wholesale into the mutual fund business. The problem with that is, many of the investors think that mutual funds are guaranteed, or insured, because they bought them through the bank. But of course they are not insured, as I have previously explained.

Truth be told, the banks have done a poor job of informing people of this fact. Because if they did inform them, their customers would go to the proper people to do their investments, and the banks would then lose that potential profit. I believe that in the near future we are going to have a big mess as these people learn the painful fact that any losses they suffer in their mutual funds are not backed up by the FDIC. That's going to be a painful realization for many.

And even though the bankers have tried to hire bona fide financial advisors who are Series 7-licensed to come in and help them, they are still going to have a mess on their hands. It is hard to have top-flight financial advisors come and work in a bank setting.

The result of this, I believe, is that the banks have sub-par people giving financial advice—essentially people who couldn't make it in the stock-brokerage business. Obviously, my advice is similar to using insurance agents for financial advisors: let the bankers stick to banking. Use a bona fide financial advisor to get financial planning.

Out of all of these different kinds of options for investors—CFPs, insurance agents, stockbrokers, CPAs, etc.—what is the best type of financial investment advisor, and why?

I think the best type is where you can get one-stop shopping—everything you need: planning, trust advice, tax advice, insurance if you need it, stocks and bonds, and portfolio management, on a fee basis. And that place is the RIA.

I realize that this is going to be a controversial issue, and that it may sound self-serving, but I believe that time will tell that my opinions are accurate on this. The biggest reason I converted my status, and the status of my employees and my firm, to RIA from a stockbrokerage house, was to better serve the client. That is the number-one consideration, and the one the investor should care about most.

Once I have chosen a financial advisor, how do I know if he is serving my needs and investing my money wisely? How can I evaluate his performance mid-stream?

Just as there are no two people alike, so also no two financial advisors are alike. This is perhaps no more true than in the investment world. Sometimes it seems that every financial advisor tells his clients, "This is the only way to do it," and people either just believe him, or don't know any better (or both), so they wind up ill-served. That's part of why I'm writing this book. Folks need to understand the investment world so they can become intelligent consumers of financial advice.

To illustrate, I had a potential client who just walked in off the street one day. My business was a stockbrokerage at the time; this was a rare situation, because almost all of our new customers come by referral; they hardly ever just walk in. But this man did; he saw our sign out front. He sat down and told me his story.

He said, "Mr. Smith, I think I'm losing money. My broker has my money invested in foreign stock funds that are going into the tank (losing lots of money). Can you help me?"

I said, "Could you bring me a a statement to show me what kinds of funds those are, so I can make a proper analysis?" He had a list with him at the time. I saw that he was with a very proper, prominent brokerage firm, one of the largest in the country, with offices just down the street. I even knew his broker personally.

I said, "It is very unusual to see a portfolio this heavily laden with these kinds of foreign securities." They happened to be tied to the European market, one with which I'm familiar. I quickly explained to him the risks that were involved and what had happened at that particular time—I think it was 1992 or 1993. Italy was trying to ratify the Maastrict Treaty. It was a rather complicated situation that I won't go into the detail about here; suffice to say that the fact that Italy had not yet ratified this treaty was having some very heavy financial repercussions. It had to do with currency futures. Anyway, these futures traders were going with the conventional wisdom that this treaty was a sure thing, that there was no way Italy would refuse to sign it. But they did refuse—and this negatively influenced the funds in which this potential client owned shares.

He exclaimed, "Why didn't my broker tell me this?" He was very upset.

I said, "Well, I'm going to bet your broker didn't know about it. Not all brokers are politically aware; there's a lot going on in the world and it's difficult to keep up with it all." He didn't know what to do, and he was heartsick since he had lost so much money in those funds.

So I said to him, "I'll make a deal with you. If you can walk down the street and ask your broker how the Maastrict Treaty affected your investment, and he gives you a clear answer, fine. Chalk it up to bad luck and hope the next deal doesn't catch you by surprise. But if he can't explain it clearly to you, bring your accounts here. We'll keep our eye on political developments that affect your investments."

He said, "That's a deal."

In about an hour, he came back. He said, "I'm moving all of my accounts to your firm. I want you to get me out of these foreign investments and get me set up properly."

It seems that what that other broker did was try to blow smoke when asked about the treaty. He said something like, "The Maastrict Treaty was some kind of treaty they had back in the early 1800s; I think it was tied to the Monroe Doctrine or something, and it never really affected your investments." Because I had educated that potential client on that treaty, and what it meant financially, I got that account.

It's so important to talk with your advisor as soon as you discover that your fund is dropping for some reason. You pick up the phone and ask him. If you don't have a satisfactory answer, then you go ask someone else until you get it. Better yet, sign up with a financial advisor who will call you first, not wait until you see your month-end statement. Communication is the key to knowing whether he is doing a good job for you—or not.

The next thing in determining whether you're hooked up with a good financial advisor or not is, does the financial advisor—or his firm—do proper due diligence on the investments they offer? 'Due diligence' is when the brokerage firm or an individual broker studies a company being considered as a potential investment. By means of this in-depth study, they decide whether the investment is too risky or safe enough for their client base.

I have made many trips to conduct due diligence on investments for my company. The president of my company, George McCuen, is a CFP, an NASD-licensed stockbroker, and an RIA. He's a very knowledgeable individual. George and I have traveled to foreign countries such as England doing due diligence on potential investments in the foreign market.

So I would recommend that you ask your financial advisor if he has ever done due diligence, or if some of his colleagues in his firm have ever done it. This would give you kind of a guideline as to where he is in the investment world. If he is just sitting at his desk and has never studied the investment from this perspective, perhaps you could do better and find another person.

One thing to beware of: you should be very, very careful acting on the advice of books which give investment advice, but are actually written by people who've never invested one single dollar for anyone else. Authors who never mention constructing a portfolio for clients are really not professional financial advisors at all. They may call themselves 'financial advisors' but they will rarely call themselves 'Registered Investment Advisors' (RIA), since that is a technical term and they can get in trouble with the government if they claim to be an RIA and they're not. They may do a lot of public speaking, they may even be on the radio. But they are really just consultants, or financial counselors. You have to distinguish between the two.

I can't emphasize enough the urgency of getting a true professional on your team, someone who is in the financial services business and active in the marketplace.

What should I do when my stockbroker advisor calls me and says, "I have a great stock you need to buy?"

Sad to say, many investors don't ask any questions when a call comes in like this; they just take the advice of their broker and buy whatever invest-ment he has called about.

Now, in a certain sense, it's okay to trust your broker in terms of tak-ing his advice—after all, that's what you pay him for. And if you have a good track record with your broker—if his advice has paid off in the past in sim-ilar situations—then fine, let him buy you whatever investment he's recom-mending. And, as we discussed earlier, give him the freedom he needs to make decisions without having to find you first by phone, if the situation warrants it.

But if you are just starting out in the investment world, or you don't know your broker that well, or you've recently changed brokers, then you should ask some questions about the investment before deciding to go ahead or not:

>> What is the commission charge?
>> How much am I going to pay for this trade?
>> How is this trade going to benefit my account?
>> How is buying this investment going to benefit me?
>> What are the risks involved?

Why are brokerage statements so hard to read and understand?

There is an opinion out there that brokerage statements are pur-posely designed to be hard to read, to keep the investor in the dark. But while there is some truth to that, that is not the whole story.

In large part, those statements are hard to understand because of securities laws, especially those governing stockbrokers. One of the chief problems is that oftentimes there are two (or more) sources of statements coming to the investor, so that the brokerage statement does not tell the whole story of the client's financial progress (or lack of it) each month. Due to these government regulations and other factors, some assets handled by the broker appear on the statement, and others don't—they are listed on the statement that, say, comes directly from a mutual fund itself, not the broker. Again, regulations and tradition are causing this less-than-ideal situation.

I'll explain these two categories (known technically as 'street name' and 'safekeeping') later on in the book. But for now, we simply need to real-ize that all the assets are not covered on the typical statement, that an investor cannot see his entire financial picture 'at a glance,' and that this nat-urally creates some confusion. So, even though the investor has all his financial dealings handled by, say, Merrill Lynch, his monthly statement is incomplete, due to these technicalities. He has to keep up with another statement that comes from his various funds, and if his broker doesn't track it—and most of them don't—he can't keep up with it, either.

What kind of solution exists, if any, for this rather confusing setup?

Our firm has tried to correct this situation by 'going the extra mile' to show more of the whole picture in one easy-to-read, easy-to-understand statement. What we do, as part of our full service component, is request that duplicate statements come to us from, say, the mutual funds our clients are in. And my people download that data into our computers every day, as they come in. Then, when we print off the statement for our clients, we will include that information as well as the information that would normally appear. That way, the client doesn't have to track two or more statements; the information from the other one is incorporated into our comprehensive statement.

Our statement shows the overall portfolio picture: listing what the person originally paid for it, tracking it as to its reinvested shares, and then giving the present cumulative value of the portfolio in dollars. This is very rare in the financial services industry. Unbelievably, most statements show how many shares of a stock the client owns, but don't go that extra step to calculate how many dollars these shares are worth. And after all, isn't that what the client is primarily interested in? He wants to be making money—not losing money—in his investment program. Sure, number of shares are important, but it's not as important as the net gain/loss in dollars. We want to supply the information that the client cares about.

Our statement is a tremendous value to the investor because he is never lost. He knows at all times exactly what his portfolio is worth. Based on that statement, we can advise the investor if he needs to sell a particular mutual fund so he is not caught in a disadvantageous situation. For instance, in late 1994 when the Fed started raising interest rates again, the bond market started tumbling. Bond funds were losing money like crazy. We're talking five-star funds that had been flagship funds being devalued. So we did a lot of hand-holding and individual counseling because people were afraid that they were going to lose all their money.

Decisions needed to be made: Do we stay in this fund? Has it lost too much value to stay in this fund? Is it going to come back? Is this person ever going to recover? etc. Without those duplicate statements coming in to us, and us reproducing that information to the customer, it would have been impossible for that investor—who has a hard time understanding what is going on anyway—to protect his investments.

In designing our statement, and deciding to tell all the important information on it (i.e., Has your account grown or shrunk in dollar terms?), we are not afraid to put our money where our mouth is. We will show the investor right up front what we are doing, and he can make a decision to fire us or continue to use us.

Do financial advisors really watch my investments conscientiously, or do they pretty much just coast once they've placed my money and trust the market to make the most of their investment choices in the long run?

Every good financial advisor has the client's best interests at heart. Therefore a good financial advisor will watch the investments conscientiously. The bad financial advisor won't. The bad financial advisor is interested in something else—probably more interested in making money personally than in the client making money.

But often the very reason why a client loses contact with a broker is that the investor doesn't require the broker to stay in touch. It's a two-way street in that sense.

We encourage contact with our clients as a real priority. For instance, I recently sent out my quarterly newsletter, *The Prudent Christian Investor*. When I send that out, I have my people call our clients. When we send out a statement, we call the client to see if he understands what is on their statement. So we are staying in touch, through the newsletter and through those personal calls. We want a consultation at least once every six months with every single client, whether it be by phone or in person. Many of our clients make appointments and come in to review their portfolios face to face. That way the investor stays in touch, too.

CHAPTER 5

How Wall Street Works

What is the stock market, and how does it work?

Ah, mysterious Wall Street. Lots of people don't really understand what Wall Street is, how it works, or what difference it makes in our lives.

Wall Street is famous for being the street in New York City where the New York Stock Exchange is located. It's a shorthand reference to the stock market.

We'll go into more detail on most of these items later on, in the chapter on stocks, but basically the stock market is a place for companies to sell portions of their companies to investors. The portions are called stocks. So Wall Street is like a farmer's market, where the farmer brings his corn and sells it to the public. It's essentially a meeting place.

The stock market had a fascinating beginning. It goes all the way back to the early 1800s in this country, although it had its roots in England as much as 200 years prior. A stove pipe manufacturer in New England wanted to expand his business. It had good sales prospects, but needed more manufacturing capacity to meet that demand. It had borrowed all of the money it could from the local bank; in fact, that local lender simply had no more money available.

So the businessman decided to ask the people in his town to loan him the money. He came up with a deal for those who would invest in his company—he offered them shares of his enterprise in return. He said to them in effect, 'If you buy shares of my company to allow me to expand, and if I make a profit after expanding, I'll share some of that profit with you. But if I have a loss, then you have a loss, too.' He found some 'takers,' people who were willing to risk some of their money on the businessman's future.

Thus he first sold stock in his company to John Q. Public, who enjoyed the prospect of making a profit in a business without totally owning the business, taking control of a business, or having the responsibility of a business. As many businesses across our nation copied that format later on, it became necessary to have a place where these shares, or stocks, could be bought and sold in these various companies. Thus the New York Stock Exchange was born.

What is a stock, and why do people buy and sell them?

A stock is simply a share of a company which that company sells to raise funds for its business activities.

Investors buy stocks for two basic reasons:

1) to obtain dividends (a regularly scheduled payments to the investor if the company has made money), and/or

2) to benefit from the equity which that stock may acquire over time (i.e., if the share price goes up from the price he paid for it, the investor may sell it to gain a profit).

Why does America need a stock market? How does it benefit us?

The chief benefits the stock market creates is that companies are able to raise capital (money) for economic growth, investors make money, people gain jobs as companies grow, and the government gains tax revenue.

What kind of magnitude does the stock market have today?

Today there are thousands and thousands of companies listed on the exchanges we refer to as the stock market. We not only have the New York Stock Exchange, we have many other exchanges, such as the American Stock Exchange. the Boston Stock Exchange, the Philadelphia Stock Exchange, and the Pacific Stock Exchange. Even up in Canada there are stock exchanges—we regularly trade on the Toronto Exchange and the Vancouver Exchange. There are stock exchanges all over the world—one very important one is the Nikkei Exchange in Japan.

All the other markets are there largely because of that one stove pipe maker, way back in the 19th Century, and also because of the enormously important stock market in the U.S., which is a big part of our economy today. Every day multi-millions of shares are traded on Wall Street.

What are all those people I see on TV doing as they run around that big building on Wall Street?

Well, that's the exchange floor at the New York Stock Exchange, and it is a very complicated place. It looks like they are in a frenzy out there—a bunch of wild people, and in reality some of them really are! The New York Stock Exchange is an exciting place to visit; I encourage anybody who is traveling to New York City to make that part of their itinerary, because it certainly is interesting.

What they actually are doing is trading shares of stock, back and forth—some selling, others buying. Some of those folks are called 'runners' and others are called 'pages.' They run to what's called a 'post' where a 'trader' is stationed. They get a price from that trader (that's what all the simultaneous shouting is all about), put it into the system, and if the price of that stock is acceptable to the buyer, it is sold, right then and there.

They are buying and selling stocks for the benefit of the investor. If the broker puts in a request to sell some stock, the actual price of that stock is determined on the exchange floor—i.e., the price is what somebody else will pay for it. For every seller there is a buyer, and for every buyer there is a seller. It is mind-boggling to think about how that works, but it does. And trades happen now in microseconds, due to computerization—whereas it used to all be done by hand. Via these frantic-looking people—and their high-tech computers—the Exchange trades millions and millions of shares each day it's open.

Do those people on that floor argue and haggle about the price?

Yes—a lot. They have what they call 'bid' (that's an offer to buy) and 'ask' (that's an offer to sell). In some ways it's just like bantering about the price of an item you see at a garage sale: you say you want X; I say I'll pay Y. Eventually you may meet on the price and you walk off with that item.

The price of a stock fluctuates, usually between an eighth of a dollar (yes, that's 12 and one-half cents!) and one-quarter of a dollar, or up to seven-eighths of a dollar. Depending on the volume of shares being bought or sold, the seller can get his price established, and then the trade is done.

Walk me through what a typical verbal exchange would be between these people on the floor.

The first trader (let's call him 'the buying trader') might say, "I have a bid for 100 of IBM at 42 and one-quarter." Translated, that means, I'm offering to buy 100 shares of IBM stock at $42.25 each, for a total trade of $4,225.

Then what happens?

Well, if that's an acceptable price to someone who wants to sell 100 shares of IBM stock, the deal is done. But if it's not, the second trader (let's call him 'the selling trader') says, "I have an offer to sell IBM at 42 and one-half." That means, I'm offering to sell my 100 IBM shares at $42.50 each, for a total sale of $4,250. He's asking for a slightly higher price per share.

So now we have a difference between the offer to buy and the offer to sell of $.25 per share, or a difference of $25 on the entire transaction. What may happen next is that either party may give in, and either buy higher than he had asked, or sell lower than he had asked. Or they may meet in the middle, at 42 and three-eighths. The give-and-take is what makes it interesting.

That transaction—trading 100 shares of IBM stock at $42.375 each (assuming they met halfway), then helps set the 'going price' of IBM stock that day. Taken together with all the other trades of the day, especially the price at the close of the trading day, helps determine the price of the share you see in the fine print of the newspaper each day.

So, therefore, most prices agreed upon during most transactions inch up or down—they don't take huge leaps, typically. Is that what you are saying?

Typically, that is correct—unless the price of the stock is going up because something is going on with the company. Something either good or bad could affect the price—like if it is merging with another company, that is typically positive and would typically result in the price going up, since the future bodes well for that stock and company. Or, the price might go down for the same reason—or a different reason—like if it declared a loss for the quarter. Nevertheless, whatever the stated value of that stock is on the ticker (a big electronic display on the Exchange floor), that will determine what traders bid for that stock.

When we hear on the television that, for example, "General Motors fell 32 points today," what does that mean?

That means that the current selling price for GM stock fell $32 per share, from the market's close yesterday to the close today—a big drop. Newsworthy stuff, especially if you're holding GM stock, but also for the economy in general. General Motors is a huge employer, and if their stock falls that much in one day, people want to know about it.

How would that fit into our typical verbal exchange on the floor?

The "going price," then, is the sum total of all the buying and selling that's going on. It consists of the GMs of the world going down in price, and the AT&Ts going up—or the reverse.

Another way a transaction happens is if I own, say, Wendy's stock. If I bought the stock at $15 per share and the stock is now at $16, I call my broker and tell him I want to sell. But I don't want to take $16, I want to make more money than just one dollar per share if possible. So I tell him I want to sell my stock when it hits $17 per share. I don't have to watch this, and neither does the broker. The broker enters a request to sell the stock at $17 into the Exchange's computer system, and when that stock hits 17 dollars, then the stock automatically is sold. What the broker did is called placing a 'limit sell order.'

There are also 'limit sell orders' going the other way if the stock's price should fall beyond where the customer wants it to. That is, the investor says, "If my stock's price goes down too far, I want to sell it, to limit my losses. So I want you to put a 'stop price' on it at 14 and one-half, because I am only willing to take a 50-cent per share loss." And so the broker puts limit orders on the stock to sell it automatically, by computer, when that price is reached. That transaction doesn't have to be monitored by a human, either.

Likewise, there are 'buy limit orders.' For instance, if a person wants to buy a certain stock, but feels it's priced too low right now, he tells his broker, "If the stock falls to $14, buy it." It's a really great system.

How much stock would the investor tell his broker to buy?

Well, the investor might either say, "Spend $1,000," or "Buy 100 shares." In the first case, the broker then translates that $1,000 into the nearest number of shares. In the second case, he multiplies the current per-share price by 100. All this is computerized, too. That way no one is going to forget to do this, or get distracted by a phone call or whatever, and the investor is covered.

Do you mean that every buy/sell transaction has to be accomplished verbally by a trader, even with the computerization they use?

Well, on the New York Stock Exchange, yes, except for the automatic transactions I have just explained. On other exchanges, such as the NASDAQ (National Association of Securities Dealers Automated Quotation System), which is the small- and medium-sized business exchange, transactions are handled fully electronically, which is even more fascinating.

When I hear on the evening news about the market going up (or down) today, what exactly does that mean?

It means that, based on the volume of trading and the average prices of the stocks that day, the cumulative total of stocks losing value or gaining value that day came out to be a net gain, or net loss, for the market as a whole that day.

Now that's different from when the newsperson says, "The Dow Jones gained four points today." We'll cover the Dow in detail later. You have to listen carefully to what they are saying, and understand the terms.

As we saw in chapter 1, the stock market is very, very sensitive to everything that goes on in our world politically, socially, economically, etc. That is part of why it rises and falls daily. If there is a euphoria about the news, then the market often goes up. If negativity dominates the news and causes a certain fear, then the market often goes down. What's really interesting is if some day's news is negative (e.g., a war is about to break out), and you'd predict the market would go down, but in actuality it might go up. That's why you need experts in there to help you understand developments; the market can be very surprising.

You may have individual stocks that are up when the market as a whole is down (or vice versa). That happens every day. But if you have a substantial portfolio of stocks that are well balanced overall, it is likely that the portfolio as a whole has dropped or risen corresponding to the market's cumulative swing that day. That's not always true, but it's true in most cases. That is why, as a stockbroker, you are interested in what happens in the marketplace and in the world at large, every day. The same should be true of an investor, but he need spend less time on the financial news if he has a great financial advisor working for him. He can sleep a little easier because of the pro who is managing his investments.

When they say on the news, "The Dow Jones Industrial Average was up 12 points today," what does that mean?

Right, here's where we are going to look at what I mentioned earlier. "The Dow" is not the same as "the market" on those news reports. The two often mimic each other, but technically they are distinct from each other.

The Dow Jones Industrial Average (DJIA) is a composite, or group, of 30 stocks that are picked out of various industries, or sectors, and these stocks are used as an indicator of how the market is doing as a whole. It's a convenient and relatively concise way to express what's happening, rather than listing the thousands of stocks on the NYSE (New York Stock Exchange) all at once. It's a sampling, but fairly reliable sampling, of the core of the market. For example, if economic news that day is good, and IBM, General Electric and Exxon (some members of the Dow Jones Industrial

Average) stock all go up, it's a good bet that the entire market will be up for that day.

So the Dow Jones Industrial Average is a bellwether of how the market is doing?

Exactly. It's like a barometer of how the market is doing as a whole.

Is it accurate?

Some experts disagree on that question, but up until now, no one has come with a better system to improve on it. I think eventually they will come up with something better, because some of it is antiquated (e.g., the word 'industrial' is less applicable to our economy today than when this list was formulated), but as of the mid-'90s, there was no indication that anything better was available.

How do companies get to be a member of the Dow?

Only the largest, oldest, and most reliable (generally, though there are no guarantees) companies in the United States are members of this index.

How did it first get invented? A board at the Exchange picked them as to reliability, size, and fiscal soundness. Additional considerations are nationwide interest among investors in buying the stock, a viable market for its products, prospects for a strong continuance of a hearty history, and other factors. They are taken off the list if their shares drop too far, or if the issuing company gets into bad business activities.

Why is the Dow so often quoted on the news media?

Because the investors, brokers, etc., who are interested in what the stock market is doing will make their opinions, definitions based upon how the Dow finishes—up or down.

Most well-planned portfolios have all or most of the Dow companies' stock in them. So it's important to the investor, and his financial advisor, as well.

When the newscaster says it is up 12 points today, does that mean $12—or what?

The Dow Jones Industrial Average is a very complicated indicator of how stocks are doing in a given day. I will try to sum it up, to make easy to understand. There are 30 major stocks used in the DJIA indicator. The following is an example of the 30 companies on the exchange, although the list changes from time to time.

AT&T
Allied Signal
Alcoa Aluminum
American Express
Bethlehem Steel
Boeing Aircraft
Caterpillar
Chevron
Coca-Cola
Disney
DuPont Chemical
Eastman Kodak
Exxon
General Electric
General Motors
Goodyear
IBM
International Paper
McDonalds
Merck Pharmaceutical
Minnesota Mining Manufacturing
Morgan J.P.
Phillip Morris
Procter and Gamble
Sears
Texaco
Union Carbide
United Tech
Westinghouse
Woolworth

When the broadcaster says this average was up 12 points today, that means with all the variation of these 30 stocks (e.g., Sears stock lost one point, McDonalds gained two), the net result was a gain of 12 points. Each point represents one dollar in price per share, so yes, that means a $12 net gain of these 30 stocks. That doesn't mean that they all went up $12, just that with all the gains and losses added in together, there was a $12 gain, versus loss. It's a composite of prices.

The DJIA can be used by the average investor by watching how the Dow finishes each day, as an indicator of the overall market. A word of caution here, though. Just because the DJIA is up or down does not mean a particular stock owned by the individual is moving the same way. Those stocks must be watched individually as to their movement.

I understand that timing is important in investing. Right? When is the best time to buy or sell my investments?

There are varied opinions on this, and some financial advisors out there will disagree with this opinion—but it's my view that the best time to buy a stock is *any* time.

Why is that?

Because stocks have had such a good performance overall. They have outperformed every other type of investment, historically. We will cover how the broker times his buying and selling in more detail later in the book.

We have all heard about the Great Crash of the stock market in 1929; certainly there are people still alive today who lived through it. But can you tell us what the details of that event were, and what the significance is for us today? For example, could it happen again?

Well, I heard an economist who said that if someone figured out exactly what actually caused the Crash in 1929, they would win the Nobel Prize. That is my opinion as well, because as much study as that economist has done on that—and I certainly have done some myself—a pat answer as to its exact cause is still not available. But if I were to give my opinion, I would say that the reasons the market crashed were threefold.

Number one, there was a manipulation of the securities market and the banking industry, wherein great amounts of money flowing in and out of the market could manipulate the prices of stocks. People were making a lot of money this way. Stock prices were being manipulated by rich people, and though I am not going to name names, they were very prominent names. These people manipulated the market and then actually profited watching it fall.

Number two, there was a drought in the Midwest, in the food basket of the nation: Kansas, Nebraska, Missouri—the Great Plains states where all the wheat, corn and the like was grown. We forget about that sometimes in terms of the origins of the Great Crash. This is the dust bowl that John Steinbeck wrote about in *The Grapes of Wrath*. It went on for four years doing the Great Depression and wiped out thousands and thousands of families who had to leave their farms and/or fire-sale their farms and move west to California to pick peaches and anything else they could find; many almost starved to death. That didn't help the economy, which was more farm- and agriculture-based than it is today.

Number three, the government itself had little to no regulations in place to prevent such a crash, like they do today. Today many rules are in place, including the SEC and other agencies which help prevent this from occurring again.

What was the significance of the famine and dust bowl to the Great Crash and Great Depression?

Even though the weather problem (i.e., the drought in the agricultural areas) wasn't related to the Crash, the weather problem created a downward pressure on the average household. It made the situation worse instead of better.

Plus, they didn't have the farm products that they were selling on the open market as they have today (e.g., the commodities market covered elsewhere in the book). What this did was to drive the price of those commodities up and make them more expensive to buy.

Many of the modern-day safeguards that we now take for granted were not in place then. In fact, many of them came into being as a result of this terrible period in our economic history.

However, it wasn't terrible in every way. Certainly it was for those farmers who became refugees. But I also want to point out that a lot of people think that everybody—every living soul in the U.S.—suffered during the

Depression. That's not true. I can remember riding around with my boss in 1968 when I was in the marketing division of International Multi-Foods. I was curious about the Depression, and he had lived through it.

I asked my boss, "How much did you lose during the Depression?"

His answer was, "We lived in Louisville, Kentucky—what Depression do you mean?" He said not everybody suffered during the Depression. He remembered buying a new Buick convertible right in the middle of the depression.

My father lived through it, too, and his family almost lost everything they had. Of course that made him very wary from that point on about taking any risk at all.

So a lot of people have a misconception about the great Crash and the Great Depression—and this is where the doomsayers are wrong, too. Those doom-and-gloom authors feel like the song "Rainy Night in Georgia"—those lyrics say that if it's raining in Georgia, it's raining all over the world. That's not true in an economic sense. Today we have ways to fix the problems that led up to the Crash, ways to keep a depression from happening—at least in the same sense it did in 1929.

In 1987, we had another crash—I well remember that day. That was Black Monday and it will forever be indelibly etched into my brain. I was a stockbroker at the time, sitting there watching the computer screen. It was October 14, 1987. I had never seen the market fall 40 to 50 points in one day. And as I watched the screen, within hours, the market fell more than 500 points. There were stockbrokers and investors all over America jumping off bridges (figuratively speaking) because their fortunes were being wiped out.

Well, there actually *were* some suicides, like in 1929, but not nearly the hysteria as back then. Family fortunes were wiped out because they didn't anticipate this happening. And then a strange thing happened. The doom-and-gloom prophets came out of their holes to tell us the near-term future.

Doomsayers, such as Ravi Batra, said that there would soon follow a depression. In fact, he wrote a book called *The Great Depression of 1990* a short time before 1990 arrived, trying to capitalize on the negativity of the fall of the market in '87. But such a depression never materialized. In fact, three months after the market fell, there was no provable adverse effect on the economy at all. The economy quickly recovered and the people who stayed put and didn't panic or jump off the bridge did too—they profited greatly as we had a boom for the three years following Black Monday.

The reason for this wonderful bounce-back by our economy is

based on all the financial rules and new laws that were put in place back at the end of the Depression. Among other factors, these included the Investment Act of 1940, the creation of the Securities & Exchange Commission, the NASD and others. They were created as circuit breakers and safeguards against a possible future crash, and in the ensuing time they have shown their value.

In the '40s, the government put these and other circuit breakers in place, which act like an internal combustion engine's heat sensor: if it gets too hot, it shuts itself down. This prevents the marketplace from falling totally apart, as in 1929. And following Black Monday, the government and the marketplace put new, additional circuit breakers into place.

Also following the Great Crash of '29, the banking industry was regulated so the banks wouldn't 'crash and burn,' like they did back then. An interesting thing to note is why we have banking holidays corresponding to national holidays. They didn't have this arrangement until the Great Depression. It keeps the people from making 'runs on the bank.' (A run on the bank is when people flood into the banks at the same time, to withdraw their deposits all at once, like happened in the movie, "It's a Wonderful Life.") So now periodically the banks shut down in order to recoup themselves, and so that if some negative news happens to hit the country that day, the banks are not open. And on those days when some bad news might cause a run on the banks, the government will be open, to help out the banks or whatever type of coordination might be necessary. That is why every single bank in America shuts down on national holidays.

From time to time I hear about various stock exchanges, such as the New York Stock Exchange (NYSE), such as NASDAQ, or the American Stock Exchange (AMEX). What are these stock exchanges, what are the differences between them, and what difference should it make to me as an investor?

There are basically three of these markets. The first market is the best known, the New York Stock Exchange, which I've already discussed.

Next is the American Stock Exchange. This is a large exchange, though not nearly quite as large as the NYSE.

The next one is the OTC market, which means Over The Counter. This is a system of telephone and computer connections between the brokers. The OTC market is also called the NASDAQ market. The Over The Counter market is the place that companies which can't qualify to list their stock at the New York Stock Exchange can get it done. The usual problem with qualifying for the NYSE is size of the company. So the NASDAQ winds up being where the small and mid-sized companies sell their stocks. This exchange has been growing like crazy lately, and can be a good place to invest.

A simple way to understand the difference between the New York Stock Exchange and NASDAQ would be: NYSE would be like Neiman-Marcus and NASDAQ would be like Wal-Mart. One is full-service, glitzy, old, and prestigious; the other is utilitarian, younger and less glitzy.

You have already mentioned some examples of the blue chips stocks listed on the NYSE, such as Exxon, GE, GM, etc. What are some examples of NASDAQ - listed stocks?

Three examples of NASDAQ stocks would be Intel, Microsoft, and Apple Computer—these, of course, are all technology stocks. Some non-technology examples are: National Gypsum, Fresh Choice, and Boston Chicken.

What is involved in meeting the criteria to get on the New York Stock Exchange?

To list on the New York Exchange, the market value of the publicly held shares must be a minimum of $18 million. There has to be a minimum of 1.1 million shares publicly held. There must be at least 2,000 stockholders holding 100 shares, and other technical requirements like these. Additionally, the company's pretax earnings must be $2.5 million in the last fiscal year and at least $2 million for the preceding two years. So that would eliminate most of the companies in America. There is no way they could sell their stock on the NYSE; that is why NASDAQ was formed.

In contrast, the smaller companies on the NASDAQ system must have $2 million in assets or more, versus $18 million for NYSE. They must have a capital surplus of $1 million and they must have a minimum of 100,000 publicly-held shares. They must have a minimum of 300 share-holders. They must meet the criteria of the Securities Exchange Commission Act of 1934 and the Investment Company Act of 1940. They have to submit audited financial reports to prove that they can meet these criteria. So NASDAQ stocks have to meet requirements, too—just not as stringent ones as in the NYSE. They can be very good companies to invest in, and if you and your financial advisor do your homework, you can confidently invest in them.

What strategic difference does the fact that a company may or may not qualify for the NYSE make? So what?

It might be a matter of preference—that the investor would rather deal with the bigger companies because they feel more secure.

Is that necessarily true?

In a sense, yes. That is why we do fundamental and technical analysis. We do it especially closely on the NASDAQ companies because we don't know them. They are not household words. For example, you know Kodak has probably got their ducks in a row, but Mustaffah's BioTech (a fictitious company) might not. Of course, Kodak's growth is probably going to be slow, but Mustaffah and the gang might have a huge pop of growth, if they've got, say, the only AIDS vaccine on the market. So that's the risk you take—or don't take—as your strategy dictates.

On which of these three exchanges can people do-it-yourself? That is, buy and sell through their personal computer, or do it directly be telephone?

No private individual can buy and sell stocks directly. It requires a broker/dealer to do the trading. Not even on the NASDAQ can private folks do this. Not even with a penny stock (something I'll explain in chapter 7).

Only registered broker/dealers can buy and sell stocks. Those personal computer setups that seem like they are directly connected are, in actuality, being connected to the exchange through a registered broker/dealer—some investors might not be aware of that.

CHAPTER 6

Asset Allocation and
Setting Financial Goals

Why should I set financial goals? And how can I do it?

Let me answer the 'why' question first. The old saying, "If you shoot for nothing, you're bound to hit it," applies here. There are always 101 distractions that come up in life, reasons that pop up as to why you should spend your money now instead of save and invest it. Raising families, climbing the financial ladder, and all the rest. Due to these distractions and sidetracks, we need to focus our thinking on things financial—and the process of setting and achieving goals is a great way to do that.

One of the major things that a financial advisor should do in the initial interview with the client is to go over what goals the client has. If he has no financial goals, they should work together to outline some. For example, some clients may want to be able to buy a second home for vacations or retirement; they may want to finance a college education for their kids, or buy a motor home to tour the country when they retire. The more typical client wants to make sure he or she can retire someday and be able to live comfortably until he dies.

They have a certain target date (e.g., the year their child enters college or the year they reach retirement age) and so that necessitates calculating how much money they need to have put aside by X date, starting with Y amount on hand today.

I have a lot of church clients—that is, where I manage the investments of a local church, or a denomination—managing their pension funds or other aspects of their fiscal operation. Sometimes a church will come to me and say, "We've got this goal of completing a building project" and they will ask me to help them achieve that goal from a fiscal point of view. We map out a plan, and it might take them five or eight or 10 years—but they'd have a goal, and a plan to reach it. Whether it's an individual or an organization, the process is the same.

Can't I just set financial goals myself? I mean, after all, they're my goals.

Yes, you're in the driver's seat. The goals have to be personalized; what you want to do is what counts.

But I still think you need an advisor because there are a lot of obstacles and pitfalls along the way that might prohibit you from reaching your goals that a financial advisor can help you surmount. Life is filled with financial potholes, and I am there to help you avoid falling into them. Or, if you do fall, I'm there to help you find the best way out. For example, there are tax problems that might be encountered, an inheritance that should be managed well to minimize Uncle Sam taking too big a bite; tons and tons of things that could come up to derail your financial progress. So your financial advisor can help you along this path.

At what age should I begin to set financial goals?

It's never too late to set and achieve financial goals. The earlier you get your thinking straight on this important part of your life, the better. Even while a teenager you can begin to gain the right habits and thinking, such as saving for that first car. Even a child can set aside a small portion of chore money for such things as charitable giving, long-term savings, clothing, fun, etc. It's never too early to start learning these things—things which don't come naturally.

How does my age affect my financial goals?

The older a person is, the more defined his goals need to be. Because the closer that person is to retirement age, the more serious financial planning becomes. Goals for a person 55 years old retiring at 65 or 70 need to be more critically formulated than, say, a 25-year-old who is trying to put aside long-term money. That's not to say that a 25-year-old shouldn't start early; I'm only saying that depending on one's age, a financial plan should be shaped accordingly.

What is 'asset allocation,' and what is its purpose?

'Asset allocation' means putting different types of investments together, mixing them as to type and sector, usually according to a preset percentage, in each person's portfolio. As we discussed in chapter 3, it follows that old saying of not putting all your eggs in one basket.

The purpose of asset allocation is to provide diversification. The purpose of diversification is safety for the investor. I showed you a sample diversified portfolio in chapter 2, where under the C-SIS method you may put 5% of your assets in gold and silver, 5% in foreign stocks, 5% in foreign currencies, 55% in domestic stocks, etc.

By spreading your investments around through asset allocation, you limit your exposure to loss (e.g., if the Yen plummets, and you've bought a bunch of Yen, only 5% of your portfolio has suffered). By the same token, though, you've limited your possibilities for gain (e.g., if gold prices go through the roof, you win, but with only 5% of your assets in gold, you don't become a millionaire overnight). So it's a two-way street. Of course, the trick is to have either success in the right portion of your portfolio (e.g., if stocks, 55% of your assets, go up, you benefit big-time), or to have success in many areas of your portfolio (e.g., if stocks, foreign currencies, and precious metals all gain).

What percentage of my disposable income you would recommend I devote to investments?

Disposable income is that portion of your earnings left over after your 'must' expenses are met, such as housing, food, taxes, etc. It's that part of your paycheck that you can decide what to do with without adversely affecting your basic living requirements.

My advice is, first of all, start somewhere. You don't have to be a big player to start investing, and you don't have to have loads of disposable income to start, either. Even if it is only one-half of one percent, start somewhere—because you will be surprised how much you can accumulate over a relatively short period of time.

If you want to get wealthy then you have to take a lesson from the book *Wealth Builder*, written many years ago—in fact, years ago banks would pass these books out to their customers. It tells the story from the Babylonian culture, thousands of years ago. This man got wealthy basically by paying himself 10% before he did anything else. That idea—of including your savings and investment plan on your list of 'must' expenses each month, at the rate of 10%—is probably the single best key to building wealth. Spiritually speaking, God should get 10%—why not also your long-term savings and investment fund? Learning to live on 80% of your income (i.e., after tithing and paying yourself) is a great habit to acquire.

What practical approaches exist for systematic investing?

Systematic investing requires discipline. It is doing something on a set day, or at a set rate, like once a month, or a certain dollar amount deducted from every paycheck. One of the reasons that 401(k)s (a retirement vehicle we'll cover later in the book) are so beneficial—and so popular—is that they are often automatically deducted from the employee's paycheck, in pre-tax dollars. In other words, you never get your hands on that money, and 'force' yourself to save it, versus spend it. You get used to it going right into that retirement account. Likewise, some mutual funds will work on an automatic deduction from your bank account if you instruct them to do so. So every month you have that investment going into your mutual fund account systematically and automatically; you don't have to think about it or worry about it. This way your account has a better chance of growing without being interrupted.

What does 'liquidity' mean in terms of my financial management, and why is it important?

Well, liquidity simply means that you can get your hands on the money you have invested at any time. Some investments are more liquid than others.

For example, if you have a CD in the bank, you have liquid money which you can get to, even though you would incur an early withdrawal penalty if you withdraw funds before their maturation date. That is, if you've bought a six-month CD, the agreement is that you put in your money and don't touch it for six months. The bank agrees to pay you a rate of interest higher than, say, passbook savings interest. But if you touch it earlier, you will earn less interest than if you had left it alone.

If I wanted some money out of my stocks, I would instruct my broker to sell, say, $1,000 worth of my stocks. He will sell those stocks and that transaction takes about three business days to clear. So, depending on whether there's a weekend falling in there, you don't actually get the money for five days. Sometimes it can take up to 14 calendar days, but that is still considered a liquid investment.

One of the greatest misunderstandings regarding liquidity happens when financial advisors or stockbrokers sell investments to their clients, but don't make it crystal clear about the liquidity of that investment. Many brokers are sued in court by their ill-informed clients because the investor didn't understand that the investment was going to be tied up over a certain period of time, or that they would incur a substantial penalty to get out of it.

There are even some investments that you cannot get out of, period—even if you are willing to suffer an earnings penalty—until the investment matures. If you've invested in a limited partnership, you have to wait until the general partner sells whatever it bought (e.g., real estate) and shares the profit with the limited partners—which might take years. (We'll cover limited partnerships in detail later in the book.) Some of these investments have a 12- to 14-year waiting period specified up front; others have six to eight years. And some limited partnerships contain what are called 'roll-up features,' which mean that at the end of the first period of time, the general partner can actually re-do the partnership again (i.e., set up another eight-year period) without asking you for your permission, and without paying you off for the first time period! If the client doesn't understand all this going in, he can get pretty hot under the collar later on!

So it pays to do careful planning as to how much of your money you're going to tie up in what kind of investments, as far as liquidity is concerned. Often an illiquid investment (i.e., one that's *not* liquid) has greater potential for high earnings, but the trade-off is that you cannot get ahold of those funds in a hurry if you need them. So that's where your cash portion of a well-balanced portfolio comes in handy.

What is an example of a limited partnership investment?

There is a great investment called Cronos in which containers are bought by the leasing company and then leased out for use by shippers. These are intermodal containers, the kind that can be shipped on truck, rail, or by sea. They're the ones you see on TV, being lifted by crane onto, or off of, those big ships at the ports. The whole shipping industry is converting to using these types of containers, called intermodals, so railroad boxcars and regular over-the-road trucks will probably be obsolete someday.

Here's what happens in this investment: the investor (the limited partner) loans the company (the general partner) money to buy the containers and lease them back to other companies for their use. It is a 14-plus year program, but it is a very, very good program with a great track record. So even though you must wait a substantial period of time to get your money back, it's usually worth it. In many of our portfolios we have had some direct investments of this type. The nice things about this particular investment are that it is 100% cash-based, and that it pays a dividend every month.

By 'cash-based,' I mean that the company doesn't borrow any money from, say, commercial lenders to pay for the containers. So the risk factor is lowered somewhat by the fact that the containers are paid for in cash (raised from the limited partners) and, at the end of the partnership program, the containers are sold. With a setup like this, the cash flow is good, and profitability is enhanced. You'd be surprised to learn how many general partners borrow money from lenders *and* investors; when that happens, the companies are just too leveraged to succeed (because there's too much debt to start out with). It is possible that a person involved with Cronos could get back their principal if the containers appreciate in value over that period of time, plus they have gotten a dividend of about 10% on the money they invested. It's a good limited partnership.

Of course, there are some bad partnerships, too. Without naming names, I will tell you about some less-than-wonderful limited partnerships. For instance, there was a disastrous partnership in Antelope Valley, California, where people participated in the buying of raw land to be developed into housing developments. The problem was, the land was out in the middle of the desert, a four-hour commute to Los Angeles each way. True, commuters live with bad travel times in L.A., but not *that* bad! Their thinking was that homes were so unaffordable in L.A. that going out to the countryside was going to be palatable to people who wanted to buy a new home.

But they figured wrong in this case. Plus, with the recession that hit California during that time, many companies left the state—employers who were supposed to provide jobs for these new homeowners. Today the empty streets of Antelope Valley have weeds growing up through the cracks in the pavement. The partnership is many years old with no return, and the investors lost their money.

Limited partnerships file bankruptcy all the time. So they have a higher-than-average degree of risk, depending on what kind of partnership they are. I would never buy a leveraged partnership where money is borrowed by the company in addition to the money that is raised from the investors.

A good example of a company that doesn't do that—and is fiscally very sound—is one we participate in that deals with what's called 'triple net leases.' Those are great partnerships. One that we invest in buys the buildings that house K-Marts, Payless Shoe Stores, Pearl Vision Eye Care Stores, and Builders Supply stores. It pays for the buildings in cash and then leases them back to the companies that occupy them. 'Triple net lease' means that the person who is occupying the building pays:

1) the monthly lease payment (which covers the mortgage payment for the partnership),
2) the upkeep, and
3) the taxes and insurance on the building.

Thus the investors have zero responsibility in that building; their income is practically pure profit. And the occupants derive tax benefits from leasing their building, versus owning it. So it's a win-win. And at the end of the period of time the partnership is specified for, the building can be re-leased, or sold and the partners paid off. The profit depends on the appreciable value of the real estate at the time of sale.

Is real estate a good investment vehicle?

From my point of view, being an investment advisor, no. I do not like real estate as an investment. Because only inflation drives real estate values. Since inflation has been fairly low during the '90s—and probably will be low for some time to come—then I don't think real estate is a good place to invest. Plus, there has been such a correction in the real estate market (i.e., overpriced real estate has taken a hit and prices have dropped to be able to sell) that in certain pockets of the country, people have actually lost money in real estate. It almost sounds un-American!

For instance, in many areas of California, if you bought a piece of property prior to 1992, by 1995 you were in negative equity (i.e., the property is worth less than what you owe on it). That's a bad place to be; there are much better places to invest your assets.

But many people I know have made huge amounts of money in real estate. How do you explain that?

Real estate has historically been a good investment, even though lately (in the late '80s and first half of the '90s) it's not.

Let's take the period in our economy prior to 1920. Prior to 1920, real estate was just land. You owned your farm or you owned your house. It had a value and that was about it. So nobody bought and sold property to make big profits. But because of the industrial revolution in this country, the advent of the assembly line, the growth of manufacturing, and the economic whirlwind that resulted, a new buzzword entered our vocabulary. This buzzword affected not only the banking industry and the government, but it affected every single household, too.

That word is "inflation." As we've discussed earlier in this book, inflation is where prices go up and, correspondingly, the value of each dollar goes down. Inflation is the driving force behind increasing real estate prices. Real estate doesn't appreciate in value without inflation. So for 70 years we had significant inflation (especially in the housing sector), and inflation made real estate a good investment. But that is no longer true.

In 1965 I built my first house. I had a three-bedroom, two-bath, full basement, one-acre lot home in Kentucky that I built for $17,000. In contrast, that house in 1989 sold for $137,000. That's what inflation did— a gross profit of $120,000. But those deals are not around much anymore, because now there is very little inflation during the 1990s. In fact, some forecasters are afraid of stagflation, and even deflation, by the end of the decade.

What are 'stagflation' and 'deflation?'

Stagflation means there is no inflation either wa; prices go neither up nor down. Deflation means prices are going down. Some real estate economists say it could be 15 to 20 years before the real estate prices come back to the level they held before the 1992 corrections. Inflation drives real estate. With no significant inflation in store for us, it makes real estate a poor investment, in my opinion.

Is it advisable to buy real estate for the purpose of renting it out—as the land-lord?

There again, it depends on the financial goals of the individual. But in most situations, in my opinion, it's not a good idea to become a landlord for investment purposes. Because the total growth in real estate is going to be low, it makes more sense to go to the markets and make your money there, without having to fool around with being a landlord, worrying about people trashing your property, worrying about having the property empty for periods of time, etc.

To illustrate, if I own a house that rents for $900 per month, and I owe $600 per month on its mortgage, I'm coming out ahead $300 per month (not counting upkeep, taxes, etc.). That might be a good return on my investment. But if my house stays dormant (i.e., unrented) for three months, I have lost money that can never be recouped—$2,700 of lost income, in this example. That's money I'll never see, because the time is past and you can't turn back the clock to get a renter in there. Whereas if I had an investment in the stock market, it is most likely going to perform for me constantly, and not be held up if a renter moves out and I cannot find another one for 90 days.

On top of that, you have the liquidity feature: you can sell stocks instantly to get ahold of your money, but it's not so easy to sell a house quickly. It can take months—even years—to sell that particular investment.

What do you think about investing in real estate as a developer, building houses to sell as new construction? Is that a good way to use investment dollars?

Well, if you are a developer, yes. But if you are a common person, with common pockets, then development is a big, big step up—and there is a large and dangerous no-man's land in between. Many people have 'died' in that no-man's land, having become financially destitute trying to make those kinds of deals. You need very deep pockets to do real estate development, and also a specialized kind of skill and expertise that most folks do not have.

How should I manage debt? Is it okay to have some debt? When, if ever should I consolidate my debts?

It is interesting that the American people look at debt as a four-letter word (which, of course, it is!). When we transform the word 'debt' to the word 'credit,' it becomes a positive term. But debt is nothing more than credit. You can't have credit without debt, and you can't have debt without credit. What you are actually doing with debt is deferring a payment to a later, usually definite, period of time.

A lot of financial advisors hate debt. They think that debt in all cases is bad. But debt is not bad. Debt, when properly used, can be an advantage, a good tool, for an individual. You might think that consumer debt, such as credit card debt, isn't involved in investments arena, but it certainly is.

The main thing to keep in mind is that you never want your debt to be greater than your ability to pay them off at any given time. This is a detailed subject that probably deserves a book on its own (which I'd like to write someday). Suffice to say that my financial advice to consumers is: If you can't handle credit, you should not have credit. Let your credit grow only when you are able to repay.

Is insurance a good investment?

Well, insurance agents sure think it is!

But insurance is a very poor investment, in my opinion. Certainly some insurance does belong in every portfolio, in every estate plan, if it fits and the person actually needs insurance. But not everybody does. We always say, buy insurance for insurance purposes—to protect your assets, and your loved ones, in case you die. In the case of loved ones, when your kids grow up and become adults, they don't need to be protected anymore—or at least need less coverage than when they were minors. And your spouse, if you leave him a substantial estate, doesn't need to be protected from the poorhouse, either.

A good rule of thumb is to not buy expensive whole life insurance, but buy the cheaper kind, term insurance, and invest the difference (between the cheaper policy and the more expensive one) in the stock market. You'll come out ahead this way.

One time I had an insurance agent come into my office who wanted me to buy some insurance from him to put in my portfolios for my clients. I needed to educate the young man by telling him that I was insurance-licensed myself and could sell his insurance, should I want to, which I generally did not. An argument ensued as to whether insurance was a good investment, and whether everybody should invest in life insurance policies. And so I challenged the young man.

I said, "I'll tell you what I'll do. You go down the street and start at A.G. Edwards, then come up to Merrill Lynch, and then come to Payne Webber, and then come to Prudential Bache Securities, then hit Dean Witter, and then you hit us. And for every insurance policy that you can convince those brokers to put in their portfolio, I will match it, dollar-for-dollar." Needless to say, my challenge was not put to the test. My bottom line is this: keep insurance for insurance purposes and your investments for investment purposes. The two don't mix.

Is it really possible to make enough money in the stock market, and other places you describe in your book, to retire on?

Absolutely. The key is the power of compound interest. Let's suppose that I am 20 years old and I put $100 per month in a savings account at 10% interest. That is a pretty fair rate of earnings to compare to the stock market. If I did that every month until I was only 28 years old, I could then *stop* investing. I would just let the principal and interest accumulate, or compound, not taking any out to spend, but rather letting it grow and grow. *I never have to put another dime in that savings account in my life until I am 65 and it will have grown to between $494,000 and $532,000, depending on how you calculate it.* That is a lot of money for such a small investment as $100 per month.

Now, if I start later in life—say, when I am 28 years old—I must put $166 in the account per month until I am 65 years old to equal that same amount of money. If I start when I am in 33 years old, both the monthly amount and the years required to make contribution keep going up. If I start when I am 52 years old, forget it, the amount required is too high, and I'll never live long enough to make it to that goal.

That's the power of compound interest. Can you make enough money to retire by wise investing? You bet you can!

PART 3:

INVESTMENT VEHICLES

CHAPTER 7

Stocks

Earlier, you explained that a stock is a share of a company. Can you enlarge on that?

A stock is referred to as an 'equity' by those of us in the financial services industry; this is a helpful term if you understand it. Let me explain: equity represents ownership. It's the value that the person has in the company.

Just like you build equity in your home as you pay off the mortgage, you build equity in companies issuing stock as you buy their stocks. If you own a home and its market value is $150,000, but you have a $100,000 mortgage outstanding on it, then your equity of ownership is $50,000—that portion that you own 'free and clear.' A share of stock is just like that. If you purchase stock in a company for $10,000, then the equity you own in that company is $10,000. Even though it might be a multi-million dollar company, you are legally part owner. You have a say in how they do business, and own a share of their buildings, their inventory, their computers—all their assets. Now it may be a small part, but it's a part nonetheless.

How much of a voice you have depends on how many stockholders there are, and what portion of the existing stock you own. If you own more than 50% of the outstanding stock, you've got a major voice, that's for sure. But even the little guy who owns just one share has a say. He can vote at stockholders meetings and has other rights we'll go into later.

There are two basic kinds of stocks: common stock and preferred stock. *Common stock* is the basic type of ownership, and is the first kind of stock issued by a company. The chief difference between holders of common stock and holders of preferred stock is that the company pays only fixed dividends to preferred stockholders, whereas common stockholders may receive larger dividends if the company's profits are up substantially. The advantages of *preferred stock*, among others, are that 1) they receive dividends before common stockholders, and 2) in case of bankruptcy (the financial failure of a company) and liquidation (the sale of assets to pay off creditors), they receive their investment back before common stockholders. There are pros and cons to owning each type of stock are something a financial advisor can advise you on.

Besides the word 'equities' being applied to stocks, there is another technical term I hear from time to time connected to the stock market: 'securities.' How is this term related to stocks?

Most all investments are securities—except real estate, which is a tangible asset. Anything that is intangible—stocks, bonds, futures, currencies, etc.—is known as a security. Such a distinction helps you differentiate between buying a tangible asset (e.g., land or an antique car) and one that is intangible (e.g., a government bond).

What are the rights a stockholder has, once he has purchased the stock?

That is a very good question, because a lot of people think, *Well, I am at the mercy at the company now, with no rights or say-so. I just own the stock, and they benefit from my money.*

Remember, stocks are pieces of ownership. So you have rights according to how many pieces of ownership you possess. Let me give you the five major rights a stockholder has.

Number one, you have dividend rights. In other words, when that company declares a dividend (e.g., every three months they review their performance and decide if they'll share the profits—if any—with the stockholders), it is your legal right to share in that dividend. Dividends are paid on a per-share basis, so if you have 100 shares in IBM, and they declare a $.50 dividend, you get 100 x $.50, or $50 that quarter.

Number two, you have voting rights. These voting rights apply to every single equity owner, no matter how many hundreds of thousands of stockholders exist. The company calls a meeting (usually yearly), and if you want to, even with your paltry one little share, you have the right to go to that meeting with one vote and voice your opinion. If you don't want to travel to, say, Delaware, for the meeting, you have something easier, called a 'proxy vote.' That's similar to an absentee ballot in regular elections. The company is required by law to mail you an announcement of the stockholders' meeting, with the agenda clearly listed, and you can check a box as to whether you want to vote 'yes' or 'no' on these issues. Then you mail it in. They will count your vote as if you were there in person.

Number three is preemptive rights. What this means is that if the corporation is going to issue, say, a million more shares of stock, the stockholder has a right to be able to buy all, or some, of those shares before the general public can. The reason stockholders are interested in this opportunity is because many of them would like to own more of, say, IBM if possible. If a million new shares are spread out there in the market, an issue called 'dilution' arises, which matters to some investors. 'Dilution' refers to the situation where there are so many stock shares spread throughout investors' portfolios that each individual share is worth less in a relative sense. It's a kind of 'inflation' for stockholders.

Number four, the shareholder has limited liability. That is, the shareholder cannot lose more money than he has invested in that company. In other words, if the company went bankrupt, then the shareholder loses the value of his shares—his investment—but he cannot lose more than that because he has only a limited liability as part owner of the company.

Meaning, if someone were to sue that bankrupt company, they could not sue the shareholder too?

That is correct. In suits brought by creditors, it's common to go after all the owners, as well as the company itself. And a normal part-owner of a company can be liable for more than his share—e.g., say a junior partner owns one-quarter of a small company. The company goes under and creditors can get his house, his savings, and all his assets, if the bankruptcy court allows. This is not true of a stockholder; his loss is limited to the amount of his investment.

Number five, the right that is very seldom used (as a matter of fact, in all of my experience I don't know that it ever has been used): every shareholder has the right to inspect the corporate books. The idea here is that if you're part owner, no secrets should be kept from you in terms of the corporations finances. But this could get unwieldy—thousands of shareholders coming in the front door at a corporate headquarters—demanding to be shown the accounting department! So to keep stockholders from unduly interrupting the business, they send out an audited financial report that goes out to all shareholders once a year. This is called the annual report. If that does not satisfy a shareholder, the shareholder has the right to go and inspect the books personally. That inspection would be at the shareholder's expense and structured so as not to impede business operations for the company. But it is a right of the shareholder, should they wish to exercise it.

What about the fabled 'ground-floor opportunities' I always hear about in stocks? Are those worthy of investors' time, effort, and money?

Well, ground-floor opportunities open up in the form of what is called an IPO, which means Initial Public Offering. You read about them in the business press from time to time; they are often accompanied by much enthusiasm and excitement.

First of all, it is my opinion that most investors should stay away from IPOs. When the broker calls you up on the phone and he's got 'a hot new issue' that's just coming out and it's only going to cost you $20 per share, beware. My experience is that most of the time, the next day it is down to $15 per share, a 25% loss for you in just one day—bad news indeed. And it typically takes a long time for the price per share to get back up to $20—or higher.

However, sometimes the IPO opens at $20 per share and quickly goes to $30 per share, a gain of 33% for you in a short time. So it depends on what the product is. Don't buy it unless you are reasonably sure that your broker has researched it well and knows what he is talking about.

Here's an example of hitting and missing with an IPO, from my own experience. When TMX, which is Telefonos Mexicanos (the national phone company of Mexico), came out on May 13, 1991, it opened up at somewhere around $27.25 a share as an IPO. I had the opportunity to buy this stock for my investors' portfolios. However, I felt buying a stock of the telephone company in a third-world country like Mexico was too risky for my clients, so I passed it up. I didn't know that eventually AT&T would make an alliance with TMX and so when that happened (in 1994), the price of the stock went to $76 per share.

Later, in the mid 1990s, TMX had a big drop in share price, because of the Mexican peso problem. But the stock will very probably come back eventually because it is a solid company. A great deal of money was made initially with that rise, but also a great deal was lost when the peso devaluation hit in 1995. I missed the early profit-making, as I didn't buy TMX until the later years when the stock was somewhere around $35 per share, in the late 1980s or very early 1990s. But I still made a profit in the stock. However, not the profit I could have made, had I jumped into TMX at the IPO stage.

The opposite is true with a company called Cifra. Cifra is the largest retailer in Mexico. Based upon some public news that Cifra may make an alliance with Wal-Mart, we felt it was a pretty safe stock to invest in because of Wal-Mart's success. So I bought the stock at $.65 per share. I held the stock and sold most of it when it hit $3.20 per share. If an investor had put $65,000 in initially, buying 100,000 shares of Cifra, and then sold those shares at $320,000, they would have profited $255,000, in addition to getting all their initial investment back. And all that happened within six months. So there is an example of how much can be made in the market if you hit it exactly right.

But most of the time IPOs are very, very risky and you should stay away from them unless you and your financial advisor really know what you are doing—and/or you have the money to lose. Especially be careful of what I call 'bar-room brokers.' These are guys you hear from in bars, or on the golf course, or just over the back hedge at home, who give you supposedly informed counsel on which stocks to buy and sell.

The stock market is like religion. If you mention the word 'God,' suddenly everybody is an expert—whether they go to church, or read the Bible, or not—they claim to know everything about God, they are all experts about what God is doing. The same thing happens in the marketplace. You have certain people like your uncle, your brother-in-law, your colleague at work who always have a hot tip on stocks. You have to be careful from taking advice from people who are unregistered, so-called 'financial advisors'—even if they write books and give speeches.

It's like this: I go to the doctor with a growth on my face, and the doctor says, "This growth is cancerous." I go to 99 other doctors and 99 doctors tell me the same thing. But I go to my brother-in-law, who has never performed surgery, never prescribed a remedy for any kind of an illness, never worked in an operating room, knows nothing about it, and he tells me "It's not cancerous, don't worry about it." Whom am I going to believe? The sad thing is, many of us would believe the brother-in-law when it comes to the stock market. More money is lost on the tips of friends and relatives then any other tips received from people who work in the industry.

What is a 'blue-chip stock?'

Blue-chip stocks are those issued by blue-chip companies—those companies that have been around a very, very long time and are very big and very stable. They've weathered the test of time, such as General Electric, Ford Motor Company, General Motors, companies like that. They are huge, stable and the market has a great deal of respect for them.

Curiously enough, the name 'blue chip' comes from poker games, where chips are used for betting. There are white chips, red chips, and other colored chips. Traditionally, the blue chips are used to represent the most money; they're the most valuable chips—hence they are used to describe the most valuable stocks.

Should I have all of my investments in blue-chip stocks?

Well, if you did that during the period between the mid-'80s and mid-'90s, you would have *lost* a lot of money. During that period the blue chips performed very poorly for one reason or another. But that's not to say they're a bad investment; if you want something that is going to be steady day in and day out, keeps its price pretty well constant, at times has some growth and pays a little dividend, then you're not going to go wrong with a blue-chipper like IBM or 3M. Blue-chippers are going to be there tomorrow and probably will not go bankrupt like some new companies do; they're like the Rock of Gibraltar. Not too sexy, but rock-solid and steady. Depending on your investment goals, they can be a good component of a portfolio.

What is a 'penny stock?'

A penny stock is a stock that sells typically for less than $1 per share. Penny stocks are very, very risky and almost never make any money. I don't trust penny stocks. I will quickly sell them if a new client comes under my management with penny stocks in his holdings. Penny stocks don't trade on the recognized stock exchanges—you have to search through a broker or financial advisor to even find them.

What happens in penny stocks is that there is a small start-up company with some great ideas, and an investor may think he's 'in tall cotton' (in great financial shape) because he bought one million shares. Those million shares may only have cost him $10,000 (i.e., one cent per share). But the thing that thrills this investor is the idea of owning a million shares. Yet his $10,000 are at risk—generally great risk. So penny stocks are generally a bad idea, in my opinion. Look at the news and the business magazines, and you will see that the government is arresting penny stockbrokers all the time.

What guidelines can I use to buy a good stock?

Well, there are many guidelines, and of course this is the million-dollar question in investing in the market. But I'll give you some guidelines, some rules of thumb, just for general guidance. I can't stress enough that working with a sharp financial advisor is the best advice I can give here.

First, I want to know its track record in two areas: 1) its increasing (or decreasing) price per share, and 2) its dividend payment history. That'll help me predict the future in terms of earnings for the investor, though it's not foolproof by any means. I want to know what its low (lowest price per share) was for the last year, and what its high was for the year, and look back a few years as well. This way, I can get the range that the stock may go up and down over a given period of time. And I'd also be looking at whether it declared dividends at all (they're not required to), and if so, what dollar amounts they declared per share. This gives me an idea of the company's profitability, and of their inclination to share these profits with stockholders.

Second, I'm interested in the company itself and its financial condition. It's obvious that if the company is ready to go broke I don't want to buy its stock! Your financial advisor can access technical information beyond the annual report, but carefully reading that annual report is a good place to start.

Third, I want to know what stock analysts say its potential is for growth (stock analysts are people who study companies and make recommendations for purchasing of stock on Wall Street and in brokerage houses elsewhere). The best way that an investor can find the answers to these questions is to find a qualified financial advisor who would have research material at his disposal. Every stockbroker has the NASD Stock Guides, which are updated once a month. In our offices we subscribe to many research services, one of which is Value Line, which is probably the most popular among the brokers. Value Line gives every single statistic updated regularly about any company. Plus we have online service with research centers so we could find out initially about virtually everything there is to know about a stock at any given time.

Any investor needs to have these three questions answered before purchasing a stock.

If I enjoy buying and using a certain product, does that mean I should invest in the company that makes it? For example, if I think Ford makes a great automobile or truck, should I invest in Ford stock?

An excellent question. Many folks are swayed by emotional reactions to a company's products or services.

I must emphasize that you should buy a company's stocks only if the stock is safe to buy. This would entail all of the guidelines we have just discussed, and more. These are of paramount importance. But there is an aspect where the product that the company makes, or the service it provides, does properly enter into the picture.

For instance, if somebody just invented something, and you know it's going to be hot, then a person may want to purchase the stock, based upon the fact that this is a new product hitting the market at the right time. Like if a company just developed a cure for AIDS—or cancer—that might be a good reason to check out buying such a stock. But if that company is poorly managed, even though they have a timely product, it might not necessarily be a good investment.

I will give you some further examples. Sometimes with the automobile industry, if we think the automobile company has a hot item coming out on the market soon, it is going to be a big seller and that it will affect the stock—driving the price up, we will buy it. We might load up on that stock, based upon the fact that they're coming out with this new, nifty product. That may very well pay off, and even if it doesn't, if it's a stable bluechipper, so you're not going to be badly off.

Then there is the case when you discover products by accident. Take when I found Burger King. Burger King is not my favorite place to eat, honestly. In fact I hardly ever go there, but some people like charbroiled burgers—in fact, millions do. Nevertheless, I now have a big position in

Burger King stock. One day I was looking through Value Line, trying to find a stock that had a 10-13% yield (earnings) but yet had all the other guidelines to make it a good pick. Did I think I would ever find that kind of an animal? I had my doubts.

But I came across Burger King Master Limited Partnership, which is not Burger King itself, but is a group of stores owned by a syndicate. It is big enough to trade on the New York Stock Exchange as a Master Limited Partnership. And so I looked in the yield column and found out that this stock was very, very stable and was paying a 13% dividend as regularly as the sun comes out. So I bought the stock. That was eight years ago. I still own thousands of shares of this stock. It has has been through one war (the Persian Gulf War) and two market crashes (Black Monday and a 180-point drop on Nov. 29, 1989) and it still pays a constant dividend. Its price has fluctuated some, but when I started buying it, it was $6 per share. In 1996, it was around $23. It falls occasionally down to $15-$16 per share. But the facts are, even with the fluctuation in the per share price, it still pays a constant dividend.

Now, that's not to say everyone ought to rush out and buy Burger King Master Limited Partnership stock (its new symbol, under a new name in 1996, is USV), because these data may change. You should check with your broker first. But that is how you should buy stocks.

Now, occasionally, people get very emotionally tied to stocks. I've had people come into my office and I tell them that their XYZ stock is no longer good and we need to sell it. They reply, "But, my daddy gave me that stock and I'm not going to sell it."

I would urge my client, "But Ma'am, XYZ's stock is headed down rapidly, you've already lost 20% of your investment and it could get worse."

But she replies, "My daddy gave it to me, and you'll sell it over my dead body!" At that point I have to let up; it's her stock, her money, and I only give her my advice. (She can always just frame the stock certificate on her wall, since that is all it's good for!) So we have to get away from emotional attachments to different investments, and let our heads rule, not our hearts.

If I were emotionally tied to a stock, it would probably be McDonald's because it is my favorite place to eat. I'm a 'golden arches boy' and I love that company. And I am the same with Diet Pepsi. That is what I love to drink. But if these stocks are giving me a hard time—if they no longer meet the guidelines I've discussed above—I'm going to get rid of them.

Stocks are like a baseball team. You have nine players, three of whom are superstars, and the other six have to be traded now and then. If you use that analogy to run your portfolio of stocks, you will be a winner over the long haul.

What are the upsides or downsides of owning stocks, versus other investments?

Well, the chief upside of stocks is their enormous growth potential. We've already mentioned that the stock market has outperformed every other investment since 1936, including real estate. Over the 50 years roughly between 1945 and 1995, stocks have appreciated an average of approximately 12% per year. At the rate, you double your money approximately every 5.8 years.

The downside of owning stocks is that they have a degree of risk to them over, say, a bank CD. If you don't sell them on time (as their price goes down), or you buy them too high (and they never go up in price), or the company gets in trouble, you can sustain a loss. But if a person has a good financial advisor who knows what he's doing, stocks can be an extremely profitable investment.

I remember two stories concerning Coca-Cola and McDonald's. It was the early 1900s, when brokers did the IPO on Coca-Cola. The fee they normally would have charged Coke for making this IPO was something like $100,000. But they didn't take any cash. Instead they took it in shares of Coca-Cola stock, which was a very young company at the time, not a sure thing at all.

The investment firm never sold its shares of stock and to this day still owns them. The $100,000 worth of stock is now worth approximately $1 billion—yes, that's with a 'b!'

A lot of analysts believe that McDonald's is the next Coca-Cola because of the emerging foreign markets and the way McDonald's has positioned itself on the foreign scene. For instance, I stood in line in Budapest, Hungary several years ago at the opening of a McDonald's there. I waited for two and one-half hours to get a Hungarian Big Mac! At the opening of the McDonald's in Peking, which is the largest McDonald's in the world, there was similar huge interest among consumers. There are billions of people out there who love those golden arches. People will hardly ever sell its stock when they get ahold of it. They love it. And for good reason: McDonald's has recorded 119 straight quarters of record earnings—something unprecedented in stock market history.

Is it wise to hold stock certificates personally?

No, it's not. It is unwise because people do not recognize that stock certificates are legal tender if they are signed. So if you have signed the back of a stock certificate, anyone finding it could potentially go cash it out, or sell it. Or it could burn up in a house fire and you'd lose it. The best place to put stocks is a safety-deposit box at a bank. Even better, since you can't sell the stock without a broker/dealer, the best thing is to open up an account with the broker/dealer and deposit the stock with them, so that it's kept in a safe place. Then you don't have to go dig up the stock and traipse into your brokerage with it. You already have it there and all you have to do is make a quick call to the brokerage house and ask them to sell the stock.

How, physically, does the broker dealer keep these stock certificates?

They are kept in a legal depository and are carefully identified and tracked at the brokerage house's bank or wherever the depository is. They are also kept by a well-managed computer numbering system. What's called a CUSIP number is assigned to each certificate, which is a computer-generated number identifying the stock. It's somewhat like a serial number. This is the best way to protect them from fire and theft.

Actually, new stock certificates hardly ever physically exist anymore; they are only the CUSIP number. They are electronically traded now; no paper certificate exists. One will be generated if the client wants one, but it's easier—and no less safe—to just deal in the numbers, rather than the slips of paper themselves. It's just like in banking—they don't truck huge piles of currency between banks every night; they simply trade computer numbers in accounts to debit and credit clients' accounts.

How seriously should I consider investing in stocks issued in foreign markets? What are the upsides and downsides with foreign investments?

It used to be that investors were very cautious about the foreign markets because they were very volatile. And, as I discussed, we saw some of that in the Mexican peso crisis of 1995. However, today extreme volatility is generally not the case. No portfolio would be complete without some foreign securities in it. Especially promising are foreign mutual funds, like the Templeton Foreign Growth Fund. It grew like crazy and avoided bad foreign investments.

Here is the reason: of the Fortune 500 Companies (a list of the top 500 companies made by *Fortune* magazine), I think something like 165 of them are held offshore—that is, they are legally owned in other countries. So it would be disadvantageous to ignore the international scene, since it is so much a part now of the American scene. We live in a global village. So as investment advisors we no longer think nationally. We now think internationally.

How do international trade agreements affect investments?

International trade agreements such as NAFTA (the North American Free Trade Agreement) and GATT (the General Agreement on Trade and Tariffs) do affect investments in a big way. GATT covers the whole world, whereas NAFTA only involves Mexico, the U.S. and Canada.

These trade agreements, although they are opposed by many conservatives, in my opinion help stabilize the economies around the world as they cooperate with each other internationally. They also, I think, benefit us as far as worldwide recessions go; they lessen the impact on us. We will be able to offset the negative consequences by stabilization factors like the international trade agreements. My feeling is that we cannot ignore the fact that our world has been made smaller by modern communications and market factors. It's better to make advantageous trade agreements than to insist on isolationism and clinging onto the old understanding of separate countries not doing much trade with each other.

CHAPTER 8

Mutual Funds

I'm always reading about the popularity of mutual funds. What is a mutual fund, anyway?

A mutual fund is a collection, or family, of investments. A mutual fund is typically made up of various kinds of stocks and/or bonds.

They are usually designated, or grouped together, according to a certain type of investment—e.g., a bond mutual fund (made up of only bonds, versus stocks or a mixture of the two), a government bond fund (where tax-free income is the attraction), a money market fund (to be explained later in the book), or a corporate bond fund (bonds issued by companies, versus the government). Or, they can be grouped according to a certain purpose—e.g., a growth fund (a group of stocks that are intended to grow in share value over time, versus pay a good dividend), an income fund (a group of stocks/bonds designed to produce more income than growth), a small-cap fund (small capitalization, or new/small/growing companies), or a foreign fund (a group of stocks/bonds from other countries, in emerging markets). Though I've listed several bond funds above, most commonly mutual funds are made up of stocks; that's what most people think of when you mention a mutual fund.

Mutual funds allow the investor to in effect buy a large portfolio without having to invest the mega-dollars to own an actual portfolio made up of all these stocks. Plus you get the hands-on, top-flight management normally associated only with big-bucks investors. Therefore the little guy can enjoy the benefits that used to be reserved only for the 'heavy hitters,' people who invest millions of dollars.

How does a mutual fund work? And what are the advantages of mutual funds?

In a mutual fund, thousands—sometimes millions—of individual investors pool their funds to invest together through the mutual fund company itself. This way they have clout and momentum as a group. Plus, they can attract the highly talented (and expensive) professional fund managers that pick and choose the stocks, bonds, etc. for the group. And it's the expertise of these fund managers that make the difference between making—or losing—money for the group. Most ordinary investors couldn't get the attention of these managers—some of Wall Street's finest, managers with the Midas touch—because they don't have millions of dollars to invest. But taken together as a group (i.e., the mutual fund itself), they can tap into these fabulous minds each and every business day.

Investors buy shares in the mutual fund company itself, not in the individual stocks themselves. The fund then takes the money raised by selling stocks in its fund and buys individual stocks and bonds, etc. As the fund makes money by buying and selling investments, they distribute these profits in the form of dividends to the fund shareholders. Plus, the shareholders can later sell their shares to get a capital gain if the share price has risen since they bought it. So they earn money two ways.

In municipal bond mutual funds, for example, you have a special feature: you don't have to pay taxes on the earnings. In fact, most of them are 'triple tax-exempt.' Triple tax-exempt means that they pay no local, state, or federal taxes on the earnings from these mutual funds. Those funds we will discuss in the next chapter.

How many mutual funds are available to the average investor today?

In the mid-'90s there were approximately 5,000 mutual funds to choose from—enough to confuse even the best of us! They are perhaps the most popular investment vehicles available today—and one of the wisest for the average investor.

Why are they so popular?

One of the chief benefits of investing in a group, like a mutual fund allows you to do, is the diversification that you attain. One individual investor could probably not afford to invest in shares of 150 companies simultaneously, but via mutual funds, he can.

Plus, as mentioned above, the little guy can have his dollars managed by the big pros, some of the best minds in the world market.

Can any investment make up a mutual fund?

Yes, any investment can make up a mutual fund, except direct limited partnerships, and real estate—things like that. There are gold funds, silver funds and funds involving different commodities: corn and pork belly funds (we'll cover commodities in chapter 13), etc. Investors and other financial people have been very creative in coming up with many types of funds.

Are there any types of investments that may not appear on the surface to be mutual funds, but in reality are?

Yes, and one of those is 'money market accounts.' People commonly think that money market funds are like passbook savings plans, insured and all that, but they're not. A money market fund is in reality a mutual fund, with the shares prices at $1 each. Like any mutual fund, money market funds can lose value. So you have to be very careful about the particular money market fund you buy. In the mid-1990s, a certain mutual fund took a drop of two cents, and people were up in arms. So if you had a million dollars tied up in that fund at that time, you would have lost $20,000 of your principal. It's not the same as putting your dollars in the bank—they carry some risk, just like any stock market-based investment (though usually not a lot, compared with other funds).

How do money market funds work?

Money market funds have been around since 1972. They were not noticed much at the beginning, with few investors buying into them. But today, as of the mid-1990s, there are billions of dollars invested in money markets.

They pay a yield that is not that high, but is slightly higher than what you would earn in a bank passbook savings account. The company that runs the money market funds invests in what are called 'short-term securities' to earn the money to pay to the shareholders. These might include such investment vehicles as treasury bills and commercial paper (two concepts we'll cover in the next chapter, on bonds). These typically have a higher yield than what the money market company is paying their share-holders, so the company makes the difference and pays most of it through to their account holders. For instance, if they buy a t-bill yielding 4.5%, they can pay a money market yield of maybe 4%. If they make more, they can pay more; if less, less. But the earnings for the investor are pretty pre-dictable, since the yield is specified up front.

Are money markets less risky than other forms of mutual funds?

Yes, they are slightly less risky. That's because they invest in low-risk, high-yield securities, such as treasury bills. There's nobody more safe than Uncle Sam. The money market company doesn't invest in risky bonds, like swamp land in Florida; they stick with tried-and-true, low-risk oppor-tunities.

How can I actually buy mutual funds?

Well, mutual funds are sold two ways. One, you can call your stockbroker or financial advisor and he can sell you the mutual fund of your choice. Or two, some mutual funds sell directly to the public. So you can call an 800 number and purchase the mutual funds over the phone.

Is one method better than the other?

Typically, the mutual funds that you can purchase over the phone are no different than the mutual funds that you can purchase through the brokerage house. The difference would be the investment management you would get with a financial advisor (or lack of it, if you buy direct). If a big bad problem develops in the economy or the market, nobody at the mutual fund company is going to call you and tell you that your mutual find is 'going into the tank.' They want your investment to stay right where it is— in their hands. They want you to ride out any bad times with them, not apart from them. In contrast, your financial advisor will track the fund and make it his business on a regular basis to know whether you should be in— or out—of the funds. It's that monitoring—that management—that's important to have.

The commissions are the same, regardless if you buy through a broker or financial advisor, or if you buy direct. People think that when they bypass the broker, they bypass commission of any type, but that is not true. Commissions are still paid to the broker if your account is with a broker-dealer. If it is not, and you buy direct, you pay the commission or sales charge to the mutual fund company itself. So you wind up paying commission anyway.

What is meant by the term 'no-load mutual fund?'

'Load' simply means sales load, or sales commission. It is the price you pay to buy something with a salesman involved. If you buy into a no-load fund, that means that the fund is sold with no commission paid to any salesman. If it is loaded, it means that there is a commission paid for the privilege of buying the fund.

Which of those two types do you recommend?

Well, I recommend both—because there are many good and bad no-load funds. Conversely, there are many good and bad loaded funds. But probably most of the great funds, five-star-rated funds, are sales-loaded.

That's not a bad thing. There's no free lunch, the saying goes, and it's true of mutual funds, too. It's okay to pay a small fee for the expertise the company provides that will make you money. Someone has to manage those funds in a savvy way, so you don't have to do it—that's the purpose of mutual funds in the first place. Let the big guys who live and breathe the market manage your investments for you, through the mutual fund group—

you don't have to sweat it like they do. Let them get the ulcers worrying about whether the market is up or down this hour! You just go about your regular life and then sit back and look for those (possible, probable, but of course not guaranteed) checks in the mail. That's the beauty of mutual funds, and of having financial management done for you.

Investors need to be aware that just because a fund says it is no-load, that doesn't mean there are no costs involved. You don't get something for nothing in this world. There are often 'management fees' that are going to hit the account every year, even with no-loads. They don't call them 'sales commissions,' but they are costs that come out of the customer's pocket nonetheless.

Many of the traditionally-loaded mutual fund companies have come up with what are called 'back-out loads' in the industry. These have evolved as a result of the popularity of no-load funds. Here's how they work: if the normal commission charges are 5%, you'd pay no commission up front, but it's structured so that if you sell your fund shares early, you pay some commission on the way out. Say they would like you to hold the investment for five years. In this example, you're 'credited' with 1% commission for each year you hold onto the investment. So if you hold it for two years, you pay only three years' worth of commission, or 3%, to sell it. Then it backs down to 0% by the fifth year to get out. This is an incentive for the person buying the fund to hold onto the fund. In addition, many of these funds may have a small management fee, from .25% up to 1%, that is charged to your account every year.

What is meant by closed-end mutual funds and open-end mutual funds? And which kind do you recommend?

Open-end funds are mutual funds which continually offer shares to the public. So if you bought some shares in, say, the Putnam Growth and Income Fund, that fund is an open-end fund which will continuously sell shares to the public at any given time.

In contrast, with the closed-end fund, only a certain number of shares can be purchased. What that company will do is buy, say, all Mexican stocks and call itself the XYZ Mexican Fund. And you can only buy such shares during a limited time, specified by the fund itself.

I don't recommend one type over another; it really depends upon the portfolio's goals as to which one I would recommend. Open-ended funds are more popular these days, for the simple fact that they are marketed more vigorously.

What are the normal sales charges for buying a mutual fund?

Usually mutual funds will charge between 1.5% (for bond funds) and up to 8% for some equity (stock) funds; a wide range indeed. But the better funds usually charge 3-5%.

Are mutual funds risky?

Some mutual funds are risky; it depends upon what type of fund it is. But the degree of risk is offset, in part, by their liquidity. You can get in and out of them very easily. If you think their price is going to 'go south,' you can get out before they do.

People think that U.S. government mutual funds are totally safe because U.S. securities are guaranteed. While it is true that the securities bought by the funds are guaranteed, that doesn't translate into the mutual fund shares being guaranteed. Because those government securities have a fluctuating value day by day, so also the funds that trade in them also have a fluctuating value day by day. So if the bond market is getting hit, it affects the mutual bond fund too. The same is true with the stock funds; if the stock market is going down, the mutual fund is going to be affected negatively. That's because essentially the mutual fund is a giant portfolio of lots of different securities and stocks. The same thing is going to be true of an individual portfolio that is true of the mutual fund.

There is some safety in a mutual fund, in that it's diversified and usually well managed by professionals, but beyond that, the same risks apply that apply to investing in individual stocks and bonds. When you strip away the group effect, it's the same deal at its core.

Can you give us any examples of the relative safety—or volatility—of mutual funds?

Let's take utility funds. Utility funds have almost been flagship funds (funds of which the mutual fund company is proud, since they've earned enviable rates of return) because utility stocks have been flagship stocks historically. In other words, utility stocks have been very stable in price and they pay a good, high dividend—somewhere from 6% to 8%. They pay very steadily, and very seldom if ever miss a dividend because of the business they are in. People out there pay their utility bills—they want lights on in the house, or they need heat in winter—and therefore it's easy to pass profits on to the investor.

But once in a while, such as happened in 1994, the utility index (a grouping of major utilities) gets hit. Why? Well, in this case it was because in 1990 the government required environmental scrubbers to be put on the utility plants' smokestacks to clean up the air coming out of them. Some utilities, such as KU (Kentucky Utilities), which is one of the better utilities in the country, went ahead and 'bit the bullet' up front and made this very large investment of installing this new equipment. They were able to recoup their losses without their dividend suffering too much.

Most of the other companies, however, waited until almost the very end of the period given for installation of the scrubbers, in 1995. So that affected their bottom line (profits)—they started taking huge amounts of capital out of their business to buy the scrubbers. It affected the balance sheet, which in turn affected the dividend that the investors got paid. The dividends were cut severely, and in some cases cut entirely. Utility stocks at that point became dogs.

At our firm, we jumped out of utility stocks in 1993 and never bought another one (except we hung onto our KU stocks), including no utility mutual funds in our portfolios, which is our policy to this day (third quarter, 1996). So, yes, mutual funds have a degree of safety, but in another sense, you have to pay attention to them too.

Are government, or municipal mutual funds, risky?

Some of the worst investments in America are U.S. government mutual funds.

Why is that?

Because of the fluctuating value of government bonds over the long term. Now if you're buying a t-bill fund, that's different, because of the short-term maturation dates those vehicles carry. But if you are going to buy government bonds with a 30-year maturation date in your portfolio, they have a value that can be very volatile over the long haul. That is, what looks good to you in terms of an interest rate you'll earn in 1995 on a 30-year note might look terrible in the year 1,025. That's the beauty of C-SIS—you keep your time periods short, so you can adjust as the investment environment changes.

A lot of people think (we'll study this in the next chapter, on bonds) that because government bonds are guaranteed you can't lose money in government bond mutual funds. But you certainly can. Especially in municipal bond mutual funds (where towns and cities issue the bonds). What was once considered a really safe investment is now very risky, as municipalities have problems collecting sufficient taxes to cover the bonds. During the 1980s through the mid-1990s, far too many municipal bonds defaulted— i.e., didn't pay back the investors according to the terms promised.

Municipal bonds have a rating attached to them, assigned by independent rating agencies. If they are triple-A bonds, of course, they are assessed as being relatively safe. But that doesn't mean that they don't have a degree of risk. The risk in municipal bonds are put on the municipalities' ability to repay the bondholders. If the municipality gets bogged down in its bureaucracy for some reason or other, or through taxation they haven't kept up with the costs of running their city, then they default on their bonds. It happens quite a bit.

It used to be unheard of, that a city would default. Now it is actually happening?

Yes, and there are many reasons for that. For example, without naming the name of a pretty popular 'muni' bond fund in the mid-'80s, which sold millions of shares, we can see what happened. It looked like a pretty solid investment deal at the time, and that it was going to be the thing of the future, so investors by the score jumped on the bandwagon. But by the end of the 1980s those funds had lost so much money that the credibility of the sponsoring mutual fund company was destroyed—and still is, to this very day.

How can the investor know which funds are risky, and which aren't?

It's a very rare lay person who can size these funds up. That's why I continually am saying that you need a good financial advisor to be on your side. That's what your financial advisor gets paid for—to tell you what is good, and what is not.

Why do some mutual funds perform better than others?

The answer to that is management. The mutual fund is only as good as the manager who invests and picks the securities that go into the mutual fund. He (or she) decides what investments to buy, what investments to sell, and when to do all these things. That is why the performance varies. Most mutual funds are going to be made up of pretty much the same composite of stocks and/or bonds, because there are only X amount of them available. The ones that are popular and solid are going to end up in the manager's mutual fund portfolio. Timing thus becomes the key as to when he buys, and when he sells; his abilities to do that determine the earnings of the fund.

One of the greatest fund managers in all of history is Peter Lynch, formerly of Merrill Lynch. He is a household word. Peter built the Magellan Fund, which is probably the most famous mutual fund because its growth was just phenomenal—people made a great deal of money in that fund in the early to late '80s.

The Magellan Fund today, however, even though it is one of the biggest funds in history, is but a shell of the performer that it used to be, when Peter Lynch ran it. Why? The reason, I think, is because mutual funds perform poorly if they get too big. In our offices we have a rule of thumb that we will stop investing in a mutual fund when it reaches $500 million to $1 billion total capitalization.

This is because if the fund manager wants to sell off a stock in which it has huge holdings, he may not be able to do it on a timely basis. That could be bad for earnings. He may want to sell all his IBM stock because the price is falling, but by the time he can unload it all, the price has fallen further. Plus, if that mutual fund is in a family of mutual funds managed by the same company, such a sale might adversely affect the price of stocks in other mutual funds the company controls. Therefore there is a hesitancy to do what is more prudent for the investors and shareholders, holding off on a smart move for the sake of the other funds' performance. We don't like such patterns and so we get out of too large of funds to keep the interest of our clients as foremost.

What is the future of the mutual fund market?

MFS (Massachusetts Financial Services) had a mutual fund on the market since 1926, long before the Mutual Fund Act was enacted in 1940. Mutual funds have been around for a while, and the future looks good, especially as people become more educated about them. They really took off in the 1980s and boomed in the early 1990s. I expect more creative funds will come to the marketplace in future years, especially as emerging markets open up worldwide.

How many mutual funds should I have in my portfolio?

Peter Lynch says that five to 10 funds are enough.

I tend to agree. You can only have so many mutual funds and there are thousands of them out there. But they all tend to have the same type of investments: the Dow Jones stocks, government bonds, etc. So what you should do is you pick out the ones you are comfortable with, and that your financial advisor says are good, and then stick with those. They're great parts of a well-balanced portfolio, but they're not a cure-all.

What would be the downside if a person was wild for mutual funds, maybe was buying them on their own, buying them direct, as you mentioned earlier. And the person bought 20 mutual funds, or 30. What would be wrong with that?

The danger would be in not understanding what kind of mutual funds they had. If you bought 20 mutual funds, you've got to separate them out and decide if that's a good mix for you. You might buy 20 different funds from 20 different companies and they are all equity (stock) funds. So you have no diversification, because you essentially bought all the same kinds of funds. That's not wise. You should diversify with mutual funds just like you do individual stocks and bonds.

Are mutual funds for every investor?

I can safely say that mutual funds do belong in every portfolio. The portfolio is not complete unless some mutual funds are in there. For instance, if I am going to buy foreign market securities, I want to rely on a mutual fund manager who has the expertise on the international market, rather than relying on myself trying to pick those foreign securities individually.

You've mentioned that the mutual funds manager is the heart of the success or failure of the mutual fund. How can an individual investor make sure that he is hooking up with a good mutual fund manager, especially if the manager might change companies from time to time? I can't keep up with job-hopping on Wall Street, can I?

Right, you can't. The individual investor should pay little attention to the hype and promotion put out by the mutual fund company itself and go to his broker or financial advisor. Your financial advisor is tracking that kind of stuff and should know who has the track record as the better managers, and when they change employers. That stuff is reported in the trade press, which he reads (or should read). He can give you information and statistics which are readily available to him, but which are not always available to the public.

Should I invest in mutual funds offered through a bank?

In recent years the banking industry has crowded into the securities industry as a means of self protection. Their customers have been leaving the bank in terms of a place to invest savings because of the low interest rates paid by the banks. They've been flocking over to our side, coming to the brokerage houses and mutual fund companies.

But I have the same opinion that I have when it comes to making investments with folks in the insurance business. Banks should stick to making loans, handling certificates of deposit (CDs), and handling checking and savings accounts. A typical bank is just not set up for giving investment advice and planning investment portfolios. Especially in the branch banks where very low-profile people—entry-level people, or just a couple of steps up from entry level, people not trained in investments beyond a mere superficial preparation—are making investment decisions for the banking customer.

This is not right! So many people are in trouble right now because of the poor advice given in the bank lobby, given by so many would-be investment advisors. So my answer is going to be cold hard facts as I see them. If you are going to invest in the markets, go where the market professionals are—and you won't find them in bank lobbies.

CHAPTER 9

Bonds

What is a bond?

A bond is quite different from a stock. Whereas a stock represents ownership in the company (on the part of the stockholder), a bond is classified as a debt (on the part of the issuing company). A bond is essentially a loan, made by the investor to the company issuing the bond. In both cases, the investors give money to the issuing company, but it's on a different basis in the two cases. In the case of stock purchases, the company receives money from the investor and is thereby usually promised a dividend if the company makes a profit. If the company does not make a profit, there is no dividend.

A bond is the opposite of that: the investor loans money to the company, and the company promises to repay principal plus a certain specified interest, and secures that loan by the company's assets. So where the stockholder would have little or no recourse back to the company for a loss if the company goes broke, the bondholder does. Because the bondholder has his share of the properties and 'hard assets' that the company owns.

Does that include the real estate, warehouses, offices, inventory—everything that the issuing company owns?

Correct. So in that sense the bond is less risky than the stock is. Of course, in the event of bankruptcy, often liquidation (selling off of its assets) brings less than full market value, so there is some risk that you might have to settle for, say 50 cents on the dollar, rather than the whole thing. Auctions of property and equipment typically are done at fire-sale prices. But in fact, the bondholder has a stronger position than the stockholder in terms of recouping his investment through liquidation.

How is a bondholder different from other types of investors?

Well, a bondholder is the first to be paid in a the event of a default. Debenture holders would be next to be paid; we'll cover debentures later in the chapter. Then preferred stockholders are next, with holders of common stock being last in line, as we saw in the last chapter.

So there are certain pros and cons to each form of investment mentioned above. Preferred stockholders feel good about being in line ahead of common stockholders, but the downside is, no matter how much money the company makes, they will only receive a stated rate of return on their dividend payments.

At the same time, preferred stockholders are in line after the bondholders. That's why sometimes preferred stocks are not as popular as bonds, because the bond carries a lesser degree of risk, since they're closer to the head of the line in terms of ability to recoup their money if the company falls apart. At the same time, there is a common feature of preferred stockholders and bondholders: they do not have voting rights in the company like the common stockholders do. So there are pluses and minuses to all three options.

How many types of bonds exist? Which of those types do you recommend?

There are several types. Let me give you an overview.

First, there is a municipal bond. These are bonds that are issued by municipalities—cities, towns, villages—to finance projects within a city with money that they don't receive from taxation.

Say, to build a hospital, or a new road, schools, a dam, things like that?

Right. If they can't find the funds in their regular budget, they often turn to the strategy of selling bonds. That way the money comes from a source besides the taxpayers, and taxpayers are often more open to that idea.

Second, there are corporate bonds, issued by businesses or corporations. These bonds are commonly called 'funded-debt bonds' in which the corporation borrows from the bondholder (the investor), and promises a good rate of return.

What are typical rates of return for a bond?

The regular rates of return would be anywhere from 7.5% to 12%. In the junk bond market (I'll explain that below), which is characterized by higher-than-normal rates, they can go as high as 14-15%.

Third, there are U.S. government bonds and U.S. agency bonds. Those are the basic three classes, and there are many breakdowns of those different classes of bonds.

What are U.S. government bonds and U.S. agency bonds?

U.S. government bonds would be issued directly by the government itself, from the Treasury Department—they are called by various names, such as treasury bills, treasury notes, and treasury bonds. An example of treasury bonds is a GINNIE MAE (Government National Mortgage Association) bond. Examples of U.S. agency bonds would be SALLIE MAE bonds (which are based on the Student Loan Corporation), FANNIE MAE (Federal Home Loan Bank) bonds, or FREDDIE MAC (Federal Home Loan Mortgage Company) bonds.

Are there any other types of bonds which don't fit into the above three categories?

Yes, 'bearer bonds,' which are not sold very much anymore; their rather unusual name means that whoever 'bears,' or has possession of that bond can either sell it or keep it and redeem it when it's time, according to the terms of the loan. These types of bonds would be used typically for financing projects like building churches. Of course, the most common example of a bearer bond is the U.S. savings bond. Those you need to keep track of carefully, in a safe deposit box or similar, as they are just like money: if you possess it—bear it—you've got the money they represent. You can sell them or keep and then redeem them.

How safe—or how risky—are bonds?

Lots of people believe that bonds are 100% safe. Certainly you can buy an insured bond, which is very safe because it is insured by an insurance company. But most municipal bonds are not bought that way; that's where the confusion comes in. People believe that if the government sells a bond, it is 100% guaranteed—and that's not always the case.

The only bond the federal government guarantees is a GINNIE MAE bond. Yet you can still lose money in a GINNIE MAE, because it is only guaranteed if you hold it to maturity.

What does that mean, 'hold it to maturity?'

Well, when you buy a bond, it has a stated rate of return, like 10% per year in dividend payments, over a stated time period for holding onto the bond, say, 10 years.

All bonds are sold in denominations of $1,000. Here's an example: you buy one bond for $1,000 (what's technically called 'par value') with the agreement that if you wait 10 years, you'll get back your $1,000 investment, and along the way you'll receive 10% yield, or $100 per year, in interest payments. So for 10 years you get checks twice a year, for a total of $100 per year. At the end of the term, you cash in your bond (a process technically called 'redemption') to the issuing company and they give you your initial investment of $1,000 back for each bond you bought. (Investors typically buy more than one bond for $1,000 each.)

There are two cases where this differs: what's called buying bonds 'at a premium,' and buying them 'at a discount.' Let's cover the premium first.

Say the going rate on the bond market is 10%, as in our example above. Maybe company X has bonds to sell that offer 12% interest per year. They say to the prospective bondholder, "Our interest is higher than the going rate, so you're going to have to pay us more than par value [i.e., more than $1,000] to get in." So they charge, say, $1,100 to buy their bonds, on the basis that they'll be paying the investor $120 per year in dividends (versus the average guy in the first example who only gets $100). Then at the end of the term, they pay the investor back only par value ($1,000, which is what all bonds pay back at redemption time). So even though he had to pay more initially and he gets back less at the end, the investor has benefited by a greater-than-average income during the time period of the bond.

The converse is true when buying bonds at a discount. Maybe company Y has bonds to sell that offer only 8% dividends, less than the going rate of 10%. They know it's going to be harder to attract buyers than if they were paying 10%, so they offer an incentive to potential bondholders: they say, "Since our dividend is a bit lower than the going rate, we won't charge you par value to get in. Give us only $900 for each bond, and at the end of the time period, we'll give you back par value—$1,000—even though you didn't originally pay that amount." Thus the investor pays less to get in, and gets more than he paid when he gets out, even though along the way, he doesn't get quite as fat checks ($80 per year, versus the average of $100 per year).

The original bondholder doesn't have to hold onto the bond until maturity, is that right? He can sell it?

Yes, he can sell it any given day, and this is very often done. That's what we call 'the secondary market' for bonds. The process I've just described in the question above is what's called 'the primary market,' where issuing companies sell their bonds. But the secondary market is where bondholders sell their bonds to other investors. It's sort of a lateral market, whereas the company-to-investor is a vertical market.

The same principles apply in the secondary market as in the primary. If one investor wants to sell his bond that pays 12%, and the going rate is only 10%, he's at an advantage and can sell his bonds at a premium, in the method noted above. If his bond only pays 8%, he must sell his bond at a discount. Very few bonds are held to maturity by the original purchaser; they are usually bought and sold on this secondary market, as the going rate of interest changes. Investors are jockeying around, trying to be in the most advantageous position as far as earnings are concerned.

This explains the relationship between interest rates and bond prices. They have an inverse relationship—i.e., as interest rates rise, bond prices fall; as interest rates fall, bond prices usually rise. That has to do with the premium and discount factors I've just explained: if the going rate for interest has just increased, my existing bond is less attractive, so I've got to discount its value to get rid of it. And the converse is true if interest rates fall: your existing bond is now more attractive, and you can get more for it.

It's a lot more complicated than that in actuality, but those are the basic principles of bond trading, and they're accurate for understanding bonds in general.

What are the pros and cons of bonds, as opposed to other investment vehicles?

Personally I don't like bonds. I have a very, very small position in them. I don't like the way they're so closely tied to the rise and fall of interest rates. Inflation and other economic problems can have a severe influence on the bond market.

Some stockbrokers love bonds and sell a lot of them; I don't. If an investor wants something stable that will pay an income stream for several years, and doesn't care about growth, bonds are a good idea. It's a conservative way to go, and depending on an investor's goals, they might make sense. The vast majority of our portfolios include bonds, they're just not very exciting.

What are 'treasuries?' I hear that term on the news and wonder what they are.

Well, treasuries are debt securities or bonds that are issued by the federal government. The federal government is the nation's largest borrower. On the other hand, it is also the most secure credit risk from the investor's point of view.

What are the pros and cons of investing in treasuries?

Well, the pros are that they are issued by the government. So of all the bonds that you can buy, the absolute safest bonds are the U.S. government bonds.

There are very few cons, except you have to be careful with the maturity dates on bonds—make sure you hold them for the proper period of time, or you may lose money. This is because bonds vary in value.

Another significant con for them is that, apart from GINNIE MAE bonds, government bonds are not guaranteed, per se. That's not to say that it's a foolish investment, as Uncle Sam has *never* failed to pay back his bonds. But I want to stress that most of them aren't guaranteed.

The various kinds of bonds are backed by various things, for example:

>> GINNIE MAE bonds are backed by federally-backed home mortgages. So there is real estate behind those bonds. The FHA (Federal Housing Administration) and other government agencies help folks get money to buy houses, and this is used as security for these bonds.

>> SALLIE MAE bonds are backed by federally-backed student loans. With some students defaulting on their loan pay-backs, this type of bond is perhaps a bit less secure than the others.

There are other types of bonds, but these are the main ones most folks should know about. Your financial advisor can explain all the ins and outs, and which one(s) he might suggest for you.

Are any bonds tax-free?

Earnings from treasury bonds are exempt from state and local taxes, but not from federal taxes.

The only one that is triple tax-exempt are municipal bonds. That's why people buy municipal bonds. However, because of their tax-free status, municipal bonds carry a much lower rate of return then other bonds do. And, as I've stated earlier, sometimes municipalities are on shakier ground than is Uncle Sam in terms of ability to repay the bonds.

When does it make sense for an investor to buy tax-free bonds?

Tax-free bonds are generally sold to people who hate to pay taxes and/or folks who are in the higher income-tax brackets and already paying too much tax.

We buy very few municipal bonds for our clients because we would rather take a higher rate of return from a regular bond and just pay the taxes on the earnings, because oftentimes we have a greater rate of return even with taxes taken into consideration. There again, that's what you pay your financial advisor to do.

No financial advisor or broker should ever invest without looking at the tax advantages or disadvantages for the investor. But very rarely do brokers do that. It's a mistake that is made every day, all over the country, in brokerage houses. They focus in on the earnings, but fail to ask, "What tax implications would this investment have for this client?"

What are 'equivalent yields' and how are they important?

'Equivalent yields' is simply a way of comparing dissimilar investments and taking into account the tax factor on various types of investments.

For example, you might ask yourself whether you should buy investment X, which is tax-free, or investment Y, which is not. You simply figure out what kind of money you'd have left after paying taxes on the earnings from investment Y, and compare it to the money you'd earn under the tax-free investment X. That way you're comparing apples with apples, not apples with oranges. For example, if you could get a 6% tax-free bond (or bond mutual fund), you would need to get about 8% on a taxable investment to equal the same interest the tax-free bond would earn after taxes (this assumes a federal tax bracket of 28%).

I hear a lot about a type of investment known as 'derivatives' on the news from time to time. What are derivatives all about?

Derivatives are very complicated and risky transactions that basically amount to betting. They are often predicated on the rise and fall of things like currency exchange rates. Currency exchange rates are what you hear about on the evening news when the broadcaster says, "Today the German mark rose against the dollar, to 4.31 marks to the dollar."

Sometimes derivatives are okay as an investment, but they're tricky. Things can turn around radically within 24 hours. As long as the financial advisor is on top of developments, fine. But if he doesn't stay apprised, there could be disastrous results.

The financial troubles that Orange County, California, suffered in early 1995 is an example of what could happen. The county had a large amount of their funds invested in derivatives, and it got out of hand. It turned out very badly; the county went bankrupt. Also, in early 1995 Barings Bank in England went broke, losing more than $1 billion because their trader bet that the Japanese yen was going to fall against the market, and it did not—it rose instead. The bank recovered, but not without some huge, huge damage. That bank, by the way, had been there since 1629—it financed the Napoleonic Wars, and many of England's defenses, including part of the U.S. Revolutionary War. Barings was a grand old bank, but derivatives got out of hand and it came crashing down.

So should I stay away from derivatives?

No, because we do some derivatives ourselves. This doesn't apply to the typical individual investor; when we do derivatives, it is for institutional investors, like pension funds or other large groups.

Derivatives are fine if you use very safe securities with them. The point is, you as the financial advisor have to be very careful. You have to stay on top of these things at all times. It's sort of like driving a sports car at a high rate of speed on a race track: if you pay attention and are experienced, you're fine—but if you snooze, you lose.

Tell me more about municipal bonds, since they are so popular.

We've already noted that municipal bonds are so popular because of the fact that you don't have to pay local, state, or federal taxes on the earnings connected with them.

There are several types of municipal bonds—one of which is a revenue bond. The revenue bond is sold to raise funds to build something—a new highway, for example. Say it's a toll road. The money charged to use the road is going to help finance the project—i.e., pay back the bondholders.

Now the opposite is true with what is called General Obligation Bonds. These are still municipal bonds. The difference is that the bond repayment is made through taxation of the people in a certain section of town (say, if you install sewers for the new section of town) or the whole city itself (say, if they tack on a bit more property tax for all homeowners). But these bonds have a fair degree of risk if they are not insured, because the municipality may improperly manage their finances and their whole operation. I mean, if the mayor had an MBA and lot of fiscal savvy, he'd probably be working for a big corporation, not down at city hall! Municipalities default all the time on bonds, and people lose money.

Revenue bonds can carry a high degree of risk if they are not insured, even though the usage fee—like the toll road cited above—might seem to be a sure thing in terms of raising money to repay the obligation. Let me give you a classic example.

In one of our major cities, money was raised through a revenue bond sale, for construction of a toll bridge across the Ohio River. The thinking was, that the interstate was coming through the downtown and would cross the river at this new site. Well, the city planners raised the money and built the bridge, but the county planners decided they were going to route a beltway around the city, and use an existing bridge to go across the river. They would thus bypass the city.

Talk about lack of communication between governmental bodies! What they had was a beautiful new bridge, with no highway brought up to it on either side! The toll bridge never collected one dime and still sits rusting, right now, over the Ohio River because of this snafu. They could not find anyone who would buy the bridge, so therefore the city defaulted on the loan and the bondholders lost their money.

What are 'zero-coupon bonds,' and why are they popular?

The zero coupon bond doesn't pay a cash payment, or dividend, during the term of the bond, like most bonds do. The zero coupon bond operates the opposite of the regular bond. It is bought at a deep discount. For example, a $1,000 bond would cost you, say, only $500. But it has a 20-year maturity. So as you hold the bond, the interest payment is made 'inside the bond' and then the bond is redeemed for the $1,000 par value at the end of the term. So you make $500 on it, for holding it 20 years.

Why are they so popular?

Well it's a good way to save money without having to come up with thousands of dollars. For instance, back when I was a broker, the government issued what were called CABs, or Capital Accumulation Bonds. These were GINNIE MAEs which were sold at a discount. So they were guaranteed by the government to double their value in eight years and triple their value in twelve years, which was maturity.

I got on the phone and sold thousands upon thousands of dollars of that bond. It was one of the greatest investments I ever made.

It turned out great because the government did what is called 'calling' the bonds after about five years. To 'call' the bonds means to pay the bonds off early. In this case interest rates had gone way down, and the government could no longer afford to pay the stated rate on those bonds, since it was now so high in relation to the going rate. Well, actually they could afford it, but it was cheaper and wiser to pay them off early. So they called the bonds at a premium and everybody got a profit, without having to wait all those years. So we got a windfall—I wish that the government would do that again, because that was one of the greatest investments I ever made.

But why are zero coupons popular?

Because you can buy a $1,000 bond for as little as 50 bucks. And all you have to do is wait until maturity and you've got 1,000 bucks. So it's a small capital outlay, and easy to get ahead with: just wait. I buy them all the time for my clients.

The same thing is true with corporations. Corporations issue 'zeros,' too. They are popular for corporations as well as the government to issue, because they don't have to come up with a lot of money each year (to pay 10% dividends). They can raise revenue fast, and defer the payment to a later date.

What is the typical yield on a zero coupon?

It can be 12% to 14% on government zero coupons. It can be 7% to 10% if it's a corporate bond.

I have seen Government Zero Coupon Bonds have a strong yield. A few years ago I sold Capital Accumulation Bonds (CABS) which were Ginnie Maes. The government guaranteed the bonds to double in value in eight years and triple in twelve years. This represented a 9.3% return on investment, which is pretty strong for a government bond. Some Corporate Zero Coupon Bonds yield as much as 14%, but are more risky.

What is a coupon bond?

A coupon bond is commonly known as the bearer bond. This means that there's no record of the investors who purchased these bonds and the bondholder's name doesn't appear on the certificate. So it is a bond that is like legal tender. It can be given to anybody, cashed in by anybody, without a signature, or stolen—so whoever has it, has the money it represents. I own some bearer bonds from some church investments, and they are in a safe-deposit box. Churches used these more commonly back then. But today very few are sold.

What are junk bonds? I hear a lot about them. Are they a bad investment—or illegal?

Junk bonds are a very misunderstood type of bond. They are corporate bonds. The reason they are called 'junk bonds' is because they can't get the rating of a good quality bond, such as 'A,' 'AA,' or 'AAA.' So they get a lower rating—that's why they are called junk. But it doesn't mean that they're worthless. It just means they're more risky than standard bonds.

Another reason that they are called 'junk' is that they offer to pay a very high rate of return. More return than is offered by practically any other type of investment you can buy.

What kind of yield or return is typical on a junk bond?

Between 10% and 15% is typical.

But with the higher potential for earnings also comes the higher risk?

Correct. It's a trade-off.

Do you ever recommend or buy junk bonds?

People think that junk bonds have been outlawed because what happened in 1987 with bond trader Michael Milken. He was the man who came up with the concept of the junk bond, which is nothing short of brilliant. The junk bond was created because corporations which were struggling couldn't borrow any more money at the bank, and couldn't issue any more stock; they needed capital. So Mr. Milken says in effect, "Okay, we'll lure the money in by offering higher-than-average rates for bonds." And that is exactly what happened. Bond money flooded in.

But didn't Michael Milken go to jail?

Yes, and other people went, too. But they didn't go for inventing the junk bond; they went because they manipulated and misrepresented the bond market.

And by the way, I support what Michael Milken did; I think he got a raw deal from the government that landed him in prison. I think the man was brilliant, and I think he ought to be back in the investment field. It's my opinion that he took a hit for some people higher up. But that's a complicated story that we don't need to get into here.

Nevertheless, I still sell junk bonds on occasion, when I think the risk is manageable.

What's a bond rating all about, if that's what sets junk bonds apart from other bonds?

An 'A' rating would be typical of an IBM bond, and an 'AA' rating would be even less risk than an 'A.' And so on, up to 'AAA.' The rating is done by the MSRB, or the Municipal Securities Rule-Making Board.

Is there a 'B' or a 'C' rating?

Yes. You might buy a 'C' bond, but you'd have to understand the risks to do it. 'B' and above could be easily considered. There are other groups that rate bonds, such as Moody's Investment Service, and Standard and Poor's. They do the analysis of the company, and then rate the bond according to its risk.

We pay a great deal of attention to the rating on bonds when we buy them. Generally, the higher the rating, the lower the yield. The lower the rating, the higher the yield—that's why junk bonds pay so much.

Why did the junk bond market crash in 1987?

Let me tell you my story.

In early 1987 I had some junk bonds in my portfolios. But I began to get concerned—not that I have a crystal ball—that if a company would pay an investor 15% or 16% in return for the investment, they must have a problem in borrowing the money from the bank or other traditional sources. So therefore caution flags went up for me. I thought that maybe the company could be weak or in trouble.

That proved to be right, because in early 1987 I sold all the junk bonds in my portfolios. I got out because I was nervous.

I was also very nervous about the stock market at that time, although I still didn't know that the market was going to crash on Black Monday. We were in a boom at that time. But I was just a little nervous about my position. I didn't sell all of my stocks, but I unloaded the stocks in companies that I thought were going to come down in price. Overall, I got into a safer position and then the market crashed.

The junk bond market also crashed because those companies who had to issue junk bonds were a bit shaky, and couldn't survive the crash and still make those big payments to the bondholders. Payments of 15% and up are hard enough to make in good times, let alone tough times.

Why did the junk bond market crash?

It had to do with downward pressure from the economy. We had boomed tremendously, and because of that boom, companies made bad decisions. They got highly in debt, and for various reasons the prices of stocks were too high, so the stock market had to correct itself by falling.

By the way, this correction had been predicted for probably 30 years, and it came to pass in 1987.

What do you mean by the downward pressure of the economy?

Well, downward pressure means that when the prices of stocks are too high, the country is in a prosperity mode and the boom gets out of control. Inflation gets too high and then companies start having a problem making a profit. So there has to be some kind of a correction somewhere. The pressure causes a sort of bubble in the economy. If you can imagine over-inflating a balloon: if you don't let some of that air out of that balloon, it's going to pop. That's what happened on Black Monday.

What portion of my portfolio should be in bonds?

Well, most of the time we're recommending a position of no more than 25% of your portfolio, unless it's an income-producing portfolio.

Are U.S. Savings Bonds a good investment?

I think it's up to the individual investor. They are easy to understand, and that is why people buy them, plus a little bit of patriotism thrown in. Grandparents love savings bonds because they can give the grandkid one hundred bucks for a mere $25. I had a ton of them when I was a kid because every year for my birthday my grandmother mailed me a savings bond.

Like zero coupon bonds, they are bought at a discount, and then they are redeemed at face value after the years specified as the term (usually seven years). Savings bonds are different from all other government securities. They can never be used for collateral, and they are not negotiable. That means that they are non-marketable; you can't sell them. You have to cash them in at a bank, or a post office.

They're sold over the counter at a bank or post office; you don't have to use a stockbroker. You just pay cash for it (e.g., you pay $50 for a $100 bond), and your name is put on it and so it is kind of like a gift certificate, since only the bondholder can sign for it and cash it.

Let me give you two types of U.S. Savings Bonds and how they differ. The most common bonds are series EE. They can be redeemed before they mature because they are discount bonds. If they are held to maturity, they are paid the face value. But if you redeem them early, beware. Let's say you pay $50 for the $100 bond and you held it 18 months—you might get about $30 for it.

In contrast, the series HH bond pays interest semiannually. You can buy those and receive regular income. So they are not similar to a zero coupon bond, and not like the EE bond. HH bonds come in denominations of $500 and they have a 10-year maturity.

What is the typical yield on a series HH bond?

It varies according to what the government is putting out at that specific time. I would say they probably average 6% on the EE and HH.

Are they tax-free?

Yes, but only state income tax-free.

However, you can trade a series EE bond for a series HH bond and defer the taxes. So in other words, if you bought a $100 bond and cashed it out for $100 at maturity, you paid $25, so you pay taxes on your gain of $75. That's on an EE.

But if you trade the EE for an HH, then that $75 income is not taxable until you cash the HH someday. What you do is defer the tax. A lot of people do not know this. They do not even know about HH bonds, as you don't see very many of them.

How can I buy a bond?

Well, if you're buying U.S. Savings Bonds, as we said, you go to a bank or post office. If you're buying any other type of bond, you must go to a brokerage house or bank or see your financial advisor. To buy treasuries, you go to the bank.

What is the future of the bond market?

My opinion is that the bond market is going to have trouble in the years to come. I believe that the bond market will always exist, but it might not be as popular in a few years as it has been in the past.

Why do you believe that?

Because of the defaults of municipal bonds and because of the increasing degree of risk in corporate bonds—and the fact that the public is becoming more aware of the low yields offered by the U.S. government bonds. Also, a lot of money has been lost in the mutual bond funds. The mutual fund market has created this problem because people believe that government securities in a government mutual fund are 100% safe and 100% guaranteed—and they're not. Anything that is traded on a day-by-day basis is never guaranteed.

So you think that the public is going to have some waking up to do in terms of those risk factors and therefore it will drive down the popularity of bonds?

Exactly. Because of fluctuating interest rates, as books like this point out, people will gravitate less towards bonds. Many people buy bonds because they believe they are 100% safe. By giving them the information they need, educating them about bonds, they will come to their own conclusions. With interest rates going up and down, bonds are simply not as practical a vehicle to produce higher returns and profits as other investments are. But, even though bonds do produce smaller profits by means of income, they are in most cases steady returns that the investor can count on, year after year. This is not case in some more risky investments.

CHAPTER 10

Annuities

What is an annuity?

An annuity is a form of insurance, usually used as a source of retirement income.

It's really a simple idea. An investor pays a lump sum—let's say $10,000—to an insurance company. The insurance company then agrees to make regular payments back to the investor over his lifetime, or alternately over a stated period of time, starting at a certain age (usually retirement age). Let's say you're 40 years old when you make this initial $10,000 payment to buy the annuity. And let's say you can start receiving payments when you turn 60, and that the terms of your annuity are payments while you're still alive. It doesn't matter if you die at age 101—the annuity payments will still be made while you're alive. Alternately, if the terms of your annuity are payments from age 60 to age 90, it doesn't matter if you die the day after buying the annuity—those payments will be made to your heirs for that agreed-upon time period.

The advantages of an annuity are many. The chief advantage has to do with taxes. Because of the laws governing this form of insurance, you do not have to pay taxes on the earnings of the principal until the annuity matures (when you reach age 60, in our example). So the growth, or earnings, of the annuity (e.g., your annuity is invested in stocks or bonds and is earning money each year) are tax-deferred. That is, when you reach age 60 and retire, you'll probably have less income than during your working years and are therefore in a smaller tax bracket. So you'll pay a lesser percentage in taxes on the annuity earnings than you would have paid if you had received them during your working years. Thus annuities are very popular with people who want to defer their taxes until retirement years.

There are two general philosophies on annuities. One embodies the explanation I've just given above, that of the ability to defer taxes. That's the most common thinking. Then there is my position, that annuities are simply a tax time bomb—a bomb that is going to go off eventually. By deferring your taxes, you risk that the tax laws may very well change in the future, and it may *not* be to your advantage to have waited to pay those taxes. If tax rates go up in the future, you may wish you had paid them back when the annuity's earnings actually occurred.

History shows that tax laws tend to change about every two years. For instance, when Ronald Reagan was in office we had the lowest taxes in this century: 28% was the highest federal tax bracket. In contrast, during the Clinton administration, the top federal tax bracket was a whopping 39%. If you go all the way back to the Carter and Ford administrations, the top brackets ranged from 76% to 80%! So there is a huge variance in the tax laws over time, and that's why I don't like annuities. I don't like any kind of insurance products for investment purposes, whether they be annuities or other products. I think it's better to go ahead and pay the taxes in the present environment and not gamble on the future tax situation. Sure, be wise and smart, and try your darnedest to minimize taxes today (and especially try to maximize investment earnings), but then defuse that ticking tax time bomb today. I think you're better off all around that way.

So are you saying that annuities are not very good investments?

It depends upon the investor's preference, or the advice the investor gets. If you have a crystal ball into the future of the tax situation, and can count on it being advantageous to defer taxes for 20 years, fine. Of course no one has a crystal ball, but even a reasonable confidence in that situation might indicate that it's smart to buy annuities for a particular investor.

The only thing I can do is give my advice, my viewpoint. I have, at times in the past bought a flood of annuities. But today I buy no annuities, because C-SIS throws the annuity out because of its lack of liquidity. You cannot go in and get those funds early without suffering severe penalties. So if the investment climate changes, you're stuck, more or less. So from a flexibility standpoint, annuities are not that great.

What are typical time frames involved with annuities?

There are two basic types of annuities: fixed and variable annuities.

A fixed annuity is a guaranteed contract between the insurance company and the investor. The insurance company says, "Okay, for your $10,000 we're going to pay you an 8% return." The 8% return is guaranteed for one year from the date of your annuity contract. This is called the 'current rate.' At the end of your annuity contract year, the insurance company reassesses its current rate and assigns a new rate for another year, and so on. Each year the insurance company can adjust its current rate up, down, or keep it the same. This all depends on the return the insurance company feels it can safely offer its annuity holders.

Insurance companies place a limit, a guaranteed minimum rate of interest that the annuity will pay—usually 3.5-4.5%, on the account. This protects the annuity holder from earning less than the guaranteed rate if interest rates fell drastically. When the annuity matures, the person gets back his principal and interest, guaranteed by the insurance company.

Now here's the risk. Many people who buy fixed annuities believe that when the insurance agent uses the word 'guaranteed,' that means guaranteed by the government, or that it is insured in some other manner. They may be confusing this annuity's guarantee with something they're already familiar with, like FDIC insurance on bank deposits. But the truth is that the annuity is only guaranteed by the health of the insurance company.

And, contrary to popular belief, insurance companies do occasionally go broke. So it makes a difference what company is selling that annuity—this determines how safe the annuity is. If it's issued by Billy Bob's Insurance Co. Deluxe, founded last Thursday in Nome, Alaska, you'd better start worrying about whether it'll still be in business when you reach age 60. In contrast, if you buy it from an old and well-established company, your confidence factor can be higher.

So the fixed annuity, then, refers to a fixed rate of return. You won't get less earnings—that's good—but you can't get higher earnings, either—

and that can be bad. As in many other investment vehicles, there's a trade-off.

The second type of annuity is a variable annuity. A variable annuity offers the annuity holder investment options not available in fixed annuities. Within the variable annuity, you choose from a menu of mutual funds that your money will be invested in. The investments within the variable annuity might include stock, bond, money market, and in some cases, even foreign stock and bond mutual funds.

Therefore, the annuity contract doesn't have a stated rate of return; it has growth potential instead. But there's a two-edged sword here: that potential growth can be turned into a huge profit—or a huge loss. During the mid-1990s, variable annuities performed very poorly because the managers of those annuities didn't do a very good job in managing their portfolios. So there is a confidence problem now with variable annuities. As an investment advisor, I can tell you that it is very difficult to sell a variable annuity to our clients, given this bad track record and other negative factors as we see it. So we just don't buy them as a rule.

For a variable annuity, are there caps or limits set for potential earnings, or is it open-ended?

There is no set rate of return. It grows just like a standard investment portfolio, but it's managed by the insurance company. You can either earn a lot, or lose a lot, or do something down the middle.

Now, back to the fixed annuity: What is a typical rate of return on them?

A typical rate of return would be 7-8%. It varies, because some insurance companies offer 10-12%. But you must remember that the insurance company is raising money for some reason by selling these annuities. That may, or may not, raise a red flag. But it's something to consider. For example, a huge insurance company went broke in Kentucky in the early 1990s. And it was one of the very big, well-regarded insurance companies in America. As a result, the annuity holders lost their entire investment—as well as the insurance holders who had invested in straight insurance. The lesson here is: the annuity is only as good as the insurance company that is issuing it.

What are the typical sales charges for buying annuities?

Annuities do not charge an up-front sales charge, but impose a deferred sales charge (often called a 'surrender charge') on withdrawals taken within a stated number of years. These surrender charges normally begin at 6% to 8% and decline over a six- to eight-year period (although I've seen annuities impose higher surrender charges over longer periods time).

Bear in mind that annuities grow tax-deferred and the IRS places some restrictions on them. If you withdraw money from your annuity before age 59 and one-half, the IRS imposes a 10% tax penalty, along with taxing you on the earnings at your current income tax rate.

What are the some other features and benefits of annuities, versus other types of investments, that I should know about?

On the positive side, they do have some liquidity, in that you can get the money, though you have to suffer some consequences of early withdrawal.

However, a disadvantage is that an annuity has a sales charge, usually 6%. If you buy an annuity that matures in six years, you typically don't pay any commission up front. But if you cash it out (i.e., withdraw early) in two years, you're going to have your commission back down, just like the back-out sales load for mutual funds we discussed earlier. So say if the term were six years and the commission was 6%, if you go out after only two years, you might be credited 2% for the two years you stayed in, and pay only 4% penalty. That obviously cuts into your earnings.

This also puts the annuity holder at inflation risk and interest rate risk. If interest rates at the bank suddenly become 10% and he is locked into an annuity he can't get out of (without a big penalty) that's earning only 7%, then he suffers. Plus, if inflation is higher than his earning rate, he hasn't gotten ahead either (e.g., inflation is at 7% and he is earning 7%, he has only 'stood still' in terms of real earnings).

A couple other features of annuities that attract investors today, especially in variable annuities, are various kinds of perks the insurers offer. One such perk is the ability to draw 10% each year without a penalty. However, keep in mind that you will owe the taxes on the amount withdrawn, if it represents earnings. Uncle Sam is always ready, standing by, to get his cut—sooner or later, and it's later in this case; taxes are simply deferred.

Another feature inside a variable annuity is that you can change the asset allocation on a regular basis. In other words, you can specify whether you want 10% in bonds, 20% in stock, etc., both initially or mid-stream. And in some plans, you can actually pick the money managers like Solomon Brothers, or Goldman-Sachs, or other people who you want to manage your assets. Or, you could specify that your annuity be invested in specific mutual funds. Thus annuities have become very sophisticated in the marketplace as well as complicated—so there again you need the advice of a qualified financial advisor. The insurance agent himself is usually not properly qualified to give that kind of advice.

You mentioned on the front end of this chapter about initially paying a lump sum to the insurance company to buy the annuity. Are any annuities set up where you can pay in gradually?

No, not initially. You generally pay a lump sum up front, then you can add regular payments later on. That may be as low as $25 or whatever your insurance company says is the minimum for add-in amounts; it might be $100 or $250. But in most cases you have to start with a lump sum. Most annuities have either a $1,000, $2,000, $5,000 or even a $10,000 minimum investment for buying the annuity.

Should my portfolio contain annuities?

In my opinion, no. As I've explained, annuities are not a good investment vehicle. If you need insurance, buy insurance. If you want investment vehicles, use some of the ones described elsewhere in this book. Don't mix categories, even if your best buddy is an insurance agent!

I cannot tell you how many disillusioned clients I've had come to me and, when we've reviewed their insurance package, we find they've realized very little return in their annuity because their insurance agent told them it was guaranteed. Unfortunately, the insurance industry is not regulated nearly as tightly as the financial industry is. Because of that, insurance agents can say whatever they feel like saying, and they thereby create a mess.

I want to continue to caution my readers: an insurance agent is an insurance salesman. He is selling a contract on your life—stay away from him for investment advice. Buy insurance from him, because that's his field, but stick to insurance with the vast majority of agents. True, there are some insurance agents—insurance brokers—who are properly qualified to give overall investment advice, but they are very rare.

I can think of one client who had an insurance agent who sold him an annuity and an insurance policy, and then the agent changed companies and came and sold him another annuity and another policy, and then repeated that until the client had four or five annuities. He had him in four or five different annuity programs, and over a period of four years, every one of those annuities lost money. When this client came to me, he had no idea he was losing money, because the insurance agent kept telling him not to worry about it.

Did these clients actually lose money because the insurance company went under, or was it more a matter of not making much money on their annuity—that it was a poor investment?

No, the company didn't go bankrupt; rather, the variable annuity performed poorly. By and large what happens in situations like this is that the assets were never changed after they were originally allocated. When the market fluctuates, if nobody is reallocating the customer's assets, then a large portion of the portfolio can lose money. The insurance agent didn't know much about stocks and how they perform and he doesn't keep up with the marketplace—he's just out there selling insurance, so he has no capability of tracking the securities and giving his investors the advice they need.

In most cases the insurance agent doesn't explain the annuity very well. So when the person tries to cash out a fixed annuity early, he gets hit with this big penalty, or sales commission, or both. Or in the case of a variable annuity, he may find that the earnings have gone in the tank due to poor portfolio management, poor market conditions, etc. Both cases are usually big shockers. That's why I continually insist on using a financial advisor, versus an insurance agent, for asset management.

What is the future, in your opinion, of the annuity market?

The insurance companies are the richest companies in the world, so they are going to be around practically forever—and so are their annuities and their insurance agents. You are always going to be bothered by somebody trying to sell you insurance and insurance-related products like annuities. They'll pursue you in many ways, whether it be through the mail, a call on the telephone, somebody knocking on your door, or your golf buddy hitting you up for 'this great investment opportunity' known as an annuity.

CHAPTER 11

Planning for Retirement

Do I need to draw up a personal retirement strategy? If so, what is the best way to do that?

Yes, indeed. You wouldn't plan a vacation without planning your destination, your time of departure, which airline to take, etc. The same needs to be done with retirement.

Statistics put out by the Social Security Administration show that most people do not retire at the same standard of living that they had while working, largely because they had not adequately saved for retirement. They thus continued to work beyond the normal retirement years. This is not ideal, but it's the reality. A lack of retirement planning is usually to blame.

The best way to do this is to link up with a financial advisor who specializes in retirement planning, something I'll explain how to do in this chapter.

Do you have a feeling, even roughly, for what percentage of people do not retire when they should, due to financial need?

As of the late '80s, about 95% of Americans of retirement age are dependent upon some source other than financial independence to live. That might include dependence on family, continuing to work, charity, or welfare. The other 5% did some planning and were able to continue to sustain their standard of living in retirement.

So the vast majority is caught short in some way?

Right. I am continually barraged with the crying need to educate people in the area of retirement planning. I think that frankly a very big majority—perhaps 80-85%—don't do any proper planning, or enough preparation for retirement. They think they've done enough, but they haven't factored in some of the risks that exist—things like inflation risk—that is, how inflation diminishes your purchasing power over time.

Isn't formulating a retirement strategy something that I can do for myself? If I just read this book, use common sense, sit down and quietly think it through, can't I do it? Do I have to hire someone to do it for me?

I guess if you really *want* to do it yourself, you can. There are software packages out there, which are essentially calculators that you can use to do the work. Certainly you *can* do it yourself, but the issue is *will* you do it yourself? Most people have the ability to do it, but frankly just won't do it. I think the real advantage of having some kind of financial advisor is that they help motivate you to follow through with making contributions.

But isn't there an expertise factor that a financial advisor brings to the table?

Yes, obviously. There is a plethora of books written about how to invest in retirement plans and all of that. You can go through 800 numbers to open up mutual fund accounts. Anybody can open an IRA (Individual Retirement Account)—the banks make sure of that. But the real issues are: Which investment is right for me? What kind of return am I really striving for? Am I taking too much risk? Am I taking too little risk? Am I being sold an advertisement, or a bill of goods that is not right for me?

The issue really comes down to figuring out how much money you would need to put in your retirement fund. A calculator or computer program could figure it for you. But most people need—and want—an objective third party to help them make the right decisions. In most cases, it's worth the small additional expense. After all, this is your future you're dealing with!

It's often confusing for me as I look at getting involved with some kind of person in the financial industry. There are all sorts of letters following their names: CPA, CFP, CLU—all very confusing. What types of designations are best to work with as I think about retirement planning?

There are a handful of credentials out there that are appropriate to this subject.

Probably the most widely recognized is the CFP, or Certified Financial Planner. George McCuen has this credential. When you see somebody with those initials, you know that they have been certified in a pretty rigorous training program. They've had to go through a regimen of study and strict discipline to pass the exams for CFP. So you know that they are educated in financial planning manners, and a big part of that component is retirement planning.

The College for Financial Planning in Denver, Colorado is the institution that the financial planner receives his education from, in preparation for the CFP exams. The exams and credentials are issued and regulated by the Certified Financial Planner Board of Standards, Inc.

Is that a private group, or a government agency?

Strictly private. The government is not certifying them. But it's a very good designation to have. CFP is like the CPA for the accounting profession. They have their own regulatory board, an excellent code of ethics, and all the rest.

But a CFP does not have to pass government-regulated exams, correct?

That is correct.

Another common designation is called a CHFC, a Chartered Financial Consultant, which is granted through the American College. That is another very respected credential that would go through the same type of discipline and training that a Certified Financial Planner will. It is perhaps not as well-known in the public's eye as the CFP is, but nevertheless it's a very good credential because it is someone who has taken the time to educate themselves in financial planning matters.

Another one is called the Masters of Science in Financial Services, or MSFS. The College for Financial Planning offers a Masters Degree in four disciplines of financial planning: retirement, tax, estate, and investment planning. You find very few people who have pursued these Masters Degrees, but nevertheless, now you have graduate level college degrees in financial services, and their popularity is growing.

The CLU, or Chartered Life Underwriter, is a sort of basic credential in financial planning, but that is primarily in the insurance industry. This is somebody you would go to as a specialist regarding life insurance. Not to say that every person with a CLU does not have some financial planning or retirement planning credentials; but I would tend to say that CLU would be the lower end of the scale in terms of education in retirement and financial planning. The other three—CFP, CHFC, and MSFS—would be the preferred designations when working with financial planning and retirement planning.

Now of those four—CFP, CHFC, MSFS, and CLU—which do you recommend? And why?

I would probably recommend the first two, because they are the most widely recognized: the CFP (Certified Financial Planner) or the CHFC (Charter Financial Consultant). Those are the two that are most readily available, too. The MSFS is pretty rare, and the CLU should be relegated to insurance matters.

Let's talk about inflation briefly. How does inflation impact my retirement plan?

During the '90s I heard time and time again, "Well, Sherm, inflation is licked. It's very low. It's only at 3% it's not an issue any longer." True, the federal government has unquestionably done a pretty good job at keeping inflation low. But let's take a look at 3% inflation and what even this low number can do to erode your money's power when you get down the road a few years.

Economists talk about 'inflation-adjusted dollars' or 'real dollars' when it comes to this subject. In simple terms, it goes like this: If you need $2 to buy a gallon of milk today, in 24 years you'll need $4, assuming we have 3% inflation over that time frame. For example, let's say you are used to making $3,000 per month now, and you want to retire at the same income rate. You're in your early 40s today and you want to retire in your early 60s. Given the inflation effect, you're going to need $6,000 per month to attain that same standard of living that you have today. That is not an increase in income, it's the same net income, with an adjustment made for the effects of inflation.

So you see that even a mere 3% inflation rate is a very powerful number. You need to take steps today to offset its effects tomorrow.

So inflation is not harmless, even if it is a relatively small rate.

Right. Let's say inflation was just two ticks higher, at 5%. That doubling effect I just described would happen in about 15 years, versus the 24 years involved with 3%. And historically 3% is pretty darned low, so the chances are good that it could be higher. That's all the more reason to do retirement planning today.

Unfortunately, most folks do not understand the future well enough to compensate for it. Therefore they think that putting away a $2,000 IRA (Individual Retirement Account) will do it, or that if their company puts away some money in a retirement or pension plan, they've done what they need to. But I would submit to you that in the vast majority of cases, these steps are not sufficient in and of themselves.

I think that the real issue is doing your homework: putting pen to paper now, versus hoping things will work out in the sweet by-and-by. In my previous example, if you say, "I need $3,000 per month in order to real-ize financial independence," we've seen that in 20-four years that would need to be $6,000 per month. Well, once you know that, you have to ask, "How much money invested today, and in the years to come, will it take to create $6,000 per month income at retirement?"

A simple calculation would define this. At a reasonable rate of return—let's say 8%—you could determine exactly how much money you'll need to have saved and invested to generate that amount of money when you want to go play golf instead of go to work.

A lot of people think that retirement planning is just for the super -wealthy—that the average guy (or gal) really doesn't need to do this. How would you react to that thought?

It goes back to what I call financial independence. Do you want to work until they put you in the ground? Can you, or will you be able to work, until you die? Most people, even if they wanted to work until they drop, might not have that choice. There are health issues here—not everyone is going to be able-bodied until age 87.

Every person needs to do this planning, not only those earning $3,000 per month and up. Even folks who are living on a slim income now—$2,000 per month, $1,000 per month (the poverty level in America for a family of four)—need to lay out their financial future and go for it now, while they still have some options.

What about a more middle-of-the road example than a person at the poverty level?

Okay, let's look at a more realistic number. Take a family of four that has a combined household income of about $40,000 a year. In some areas of the country, it's not as expensive to live, so you might not need that much to retire on. But for illustration purposes, this will do for being pretty typical.

The first thing that comes to mind is Social Security. Some people say, "I paid into Social Security and therefore I should get back something when I retire." Some doomsayers say there will be no Social Security when we retire, but I don't think it's that bad. I firmly believe there will be something in place; whether it is the same as today, we shall have to wait and see.

But Social Security was never intended to be a complete retirement solution for anybody. Rather, it should be a supplement to other forms of income. How can you find out how much you'll have coming from Social Security? It is very easy to get the estimated numbers, by calling the Social Security Administration. You call an 800 number and they will take your data and in about 60 days they will give you a projection of what your income should be. It's just an educated guess, but it can help in planning.

The second thing you would look at is: How much is my employer going to pay me at retirement in terms of a pension or retirement fund? This takes an interesting turn, because in trying to reduce expenses, many companies are eliminating or reducing the amount of money they are putting into employee retirement plans. So that's less of a sure thing than it has been historically.

The other development is that the baby boomers who are now in their late 30s and 40s (as of the mid-'90s) have changed jobs several times and are continuing to do so. So they don't have a fully vested retirement plan ("vested" means it belongs to you) in many cases, since they haven't stayed with one employer for, say, 30 years like our parents did. Or they've taken money from partially-vested plans, 401(k)s and other plans from various employers in the past and rolled it over as they've migrated from job to job. We'll talk about these various plans a little bit later on, in looking at the types of retirement plans available.

You've mentioned Social Security as an element of one's retirement plan. During the late '80s and early '90s, there has been a lot of speculation as to whether the government is unwisely borrowing from the Social Security Fund, and whether that fund is solvent. Plus, some have predicted that there is going to be a smaller base of earners (i.e., people who pay into the fund) in 20 to 50 years, and that this is going to prove catastrophic for Social Security. What's your take on all this? What does Social Security look like, 20 years out?

I do not believe that Congress is going to be able to get away with eliminating Social Security entirely. They already have done some things to taint the system to an extent, and they may continue to fiddle with it in smaller ways. But they won't be able to slash it wholesale; I don't think the voters would stand for that.

Some of the tweaking they have done include many things, the most significant of which is, that most of us will not receive a maximum benefit until we are age 67 or 68, whereas our parents received the maximum benefit earlier, when they were 65. So they are moving the age out a little bit because of the fact that they need to account for the big bell curve of this baby boom generation. But as far as destroying the integrity of the system, call me ultra-American, but I do not believe that we baby boomers are going to hit our retirement years without Social Security. I just don't think we'll allow that to happen.

What are the different types of retirement plans available to me, and what are the pros and cons of each?

It depends on your situation. If you work for an employer who provides a retirement plan, then the main option is the IRA. Now there was a legislative change back in '86 that took away the ability to deduct IRA contributions from your taxable income for some employees. Many people read into it that IRAs are dead; that if you couldn't deduct them, why save at all, etc. In fact, none of those fears was quite true. The law read in such a way that most people could still put $2,000 away per year in an IRA and deduct it on their tax return.

The IRA is a very good way to contribute to a retirement savings plan. It's easy, it's straightforward, and most taxpayers can deduct it from their taxable income, deferring the taxes on that income until the day they withdraw it. The IRA is the best and simplest first step for most people.

Is there a simple way for me to understand what the distinction is between those employees who can use an IRA, and those who cannot?

Yes. Let's take a married couple where one spouse works and the other doesn't. Let's say the breadwinner (her, in this case) does have a retirement plan at work. If she earns more than $50,000 per year, she cannot deduct a $2,000 IRA. If that breadwinner earns less than $40,000, she can deduct the full $2,000 IRA. If she earns between $40,000 and $50,000, she is in what's called the phase out. Say she earns $45,000—halfway between $40,000 and $50,000. In this case she can deduct one-half of the $2,000 IRA, or $1,000.

Do you anticipate that this regulation will stay in place for the near and long term?

Well, when this book went to press in fall 1996, this was the law then. They were already talking about some changes within the IRA issue— e.g., raising that limit from $50,000 up to maybe $70,000 or $80,000 for a married couple. This would prompt more people to save for retirement through IRAs. The whole idea of the Individual Retirement Account was for Congress to encourage people to save for their own future, and not depend on the state, Social Security, or welfare. So I think government shoots itself in the foot when they take an IRA deduction away because it sends the message that 'if you make more than a certain amount, you don't need to save.' That's just not true.

Are there any costs to the investor in making an IRA contribution, or maintaining an IRA account during the working years?

In some cases there are what are called custodial fees. In most cases, though, they are very minimal compared to the benefits you receive. It might be $10 per year.

Some institutions won't charge you any fee as long as you put your money in their institution. Perhaps a bank, or in some cases a mutual fund company, will offer a fee-free IRA. If you get very sophisticated and you want a lot of different investment options and so forth, there is what is called a self-directed IRA, which takes more work on the part of the institution. In that case you could have custodial fees of $40 to $60 or more per year.

I understand that there are various vehicles that people can use for their IRA. Is that true?

Correct. There are a myriad of options.

I guess the most basic, simple one is working with a bank. In many cases between about January and April 15th, all over bank windows is painted, "Come open your IRA with us." They will usually offer an attractive rate of return because they think most people will keep the money there for a long period of time. So a bank is an easy and readily available option.

That time frame, January 1 to April 15, is important because money which is deposited before tax day, April 15, can apply to the previous tax year.

One of the advantages of doing an IRA in a bank is that you know what kind of interest rate you are going to receive. The downside of that is that there is no potential for growth beyond what the bank will guarantee. In most cases somebody who is saving for retirement may want an investment that would exceed what the bank pays.

Are funds placed in an IRA guaranteed in any way?

When placed in a bank, they are normally insured by the FDIC up to $100,000. Other forms of investment have varying degrees of guarantees.

Okay, so banks are the most obvious form of an IRA. What else is there?

Mutual funds are another very good option. Now here you open up a full array of investment options because you can have growth mutual funds, bond mutual funds, money market funds, international funds, and other forms of mutual funds, like we discussed in the mutual fund chapter. These are, in my opinion, a more viable resource for retirement savings because now you are investing with a rate of return that is going to be predicated on the performance of the mutual fund market, which in most cases in the long term outperforms the rate of return you can get in banks.

What are the tax considerations of an IRA?

Let's take the example of you putting your $2,000 in an IRA each year. Let's assume you can deduct that $2,000 from your taxable income each year. Let's say you're in a 28% federal tax bracket; you will save 28% of that $2,000, or $560, for every full annual IRA contribution. In essence that $560 is money that would have otherwise been paid to the IRS.

Additionally, you have the tax-deferred aspect of IRAs, just like we saw in the annuities chapter. You don't have to pay taxes on it when you're working, and supposedly in a higher tax bracket than when you're retired. You pay the taxes when you withdraw and hopefully you'll be in a lower tax bracket then. This is not always the case, but at least you control when you want to take the income from your IRA. You are then able to determine how much income that you are willing to pay taxes on, in any given year.

What other tax situations apply to IRAs?

In most states you can deduct the $2,000 from your state taxable income as well. Whatever state income bracket you are in, of course, you would save that amount, just like we saw in the federal case. This does not apply to local taxes, however.

Okay, back to the types of IRAs that are available . We covered banks, we covered mutual funds, what else exists?

You can put your IRA in limited partnerships, in stocks, bonds, in real estate investment trusts, and most of the things that you would normally invest in—what are called intangible investments. You could not put an

IRA in, say, a rental house.

Are there any significant misconceptions about IRAs that I should know about?

I think for the most part your financial planner would be able to keep you away from those things that you really couldn't use. And regarding the law that says who can, and who cannot, open an IRA, the financial planner is a good source for understanding that, too.

Among the various optional investment vehicles that we have mentioned for my IRA, which are safe and which are risky?

Of course your bank account is not at risk of losing the principal or interest, up to $100,000. The mutual fund is at risk, of course, since the fund value could go down and you could have a loss of principal and any growth that it could have obtained.

But the real issue of risk really has to do with the question, "What is it that I am investing for?" If you are investing for the long term, the issue that we've already discussed is the risk that your investments don't keep pace with inflation and taxes. So the risk now becomes a different element. And therefore the banks carry an element of risk if they don't grow fast enough.

When exactly should I start to withdraw my IRA money?

The IRS is going to have its day of reckoning, sooner or later. They have simply deferred the date that you have to pay taxes on this money, they have not excused your tax obligation.

The simplest answer to that is, if you're taking your IRA out beyond age 59 and one-half, every dollar you take out is going to be taxable to you at that time. This is how it's set up.

If you take it out before that age, you pay a 10% penalty, plus the taxes dictated by your tax bracket you're in during the year you withdraw. That can be a pretty stiff penalty: if you're in the 38% tax bracket, add in that extra 10% and you're talking 48%—or almost half of your money going to Uncle Sam! That's not a good idea for most people.

If you are one of the fortunate few who can say at age 59 and one-half, "I don't need that money now; I want to allow that to grow, tax-deferred, as long as I possibly can," the IRS says there is a limit to that. In the year after you turn 70 and one-half, you have to start taking what is called a 'minimum distribution' on your IRA account.

Meaning, start taking some of that money out of there? Because the tax man wants his bite?

Right—and there is a number that has to be calculated to figure out how much that minimum distribution is. At that point you're taxed on the amount that you take out.

In addition to the IRA, what other types of retirement plans are available?

If you are a self-employed individual—and more and more people these days have either a side business or are fully self-employed—there is a special option available. Instead of having a maximum $2,000 limit (as in the IRA), you can open up what is called a SEP, or Simplified Employee Pension, that will allow up to a maximum of $30,000 contribution yearly. That's a cap; the ordinary contribution is calculated below, as a percentage of net self-employed income (i.e., income after business expenses).

Is the SEP for people who are wholly self-employed, or does it also include people who are employees and also do a side business?

It covers both types of persons. You can work as an employee and for your side business, you could have that SEP account. Now the issue here is that your SEP contribution is measured as a maximum percentage of the self-employed income. It's complicated in the details, but a good rule of thumb is that your maximum is about 15% of your net self-employed income. For example, if you take in $50,000 on your self-employed business, but you net $30,000, then you would take about 15% of the $30,000, or $4,500 as the maximum amount you could contribute to your SEP. So you can see that it's much higher than the IRAs allow. There are certainly other considerations that you would have to factor in to develop this plan, and there are ways of legally increasing the amount that you can put into these plans by perhaps marrying a couple of plans together.

Another very popular plan for self-employed people is called

KEOGH. These plans can be used in conjunction with the SEP plan. Thus you can again increase the amount of money that a self-employed individual could contribute. Perhaps you could contribute closer to 25% of self-employed income by marrying these plans together.

Remember, these types of things should be done with a qualified financial advisor—most people would not want to tackle this on their own. Nevertheless, they are not so complicated that you could not take care of it with some diligent preparation. Your accountant could even give you the contribution limits and then you could go to an investment advisor or bank, etc., and they could open up the account for you. It's just that you would probably rest easier with a qualified financial advisor helping you with it.

Are there any other retirement plans that are available to me?

Another one that is very popular is called a 401(k) plan. This is called a 'defined contribution plan.' This basically is a plan established by an employer that allows pretax employee contributions. Pretax means that the money is taken out of the employee's pay before income tax withholding is calculated, effectively making that part of his salary tax-deferred. Just like with the IRA, the employee needs to pay the tax on this money only when he withdraws it, hopefully in retirement years and at a better tax bracket.

In most cases the employer will also contribute to the fund, as a means of encouraging savings for the employee.

Is that where the employee makes a contribution and sometimes the employer either matches, or contributes in some other ratio, like 2-to-1, or one-half-to-1?

Yes, indeed. That would mean, for example, that for every dollar the employee puts in, the employer would put in a dollar (in the case of 1-to-1 matching contributions). It's a very nice arrangement for an employee to have; he gets 'instant growth' on his retirement savings (assuming that the employer's contribution is fully vested immediately—more on that later).

What investment vehicles are available for the 401(k)?

The employer who establishes the plan will normally have a menu of different investment options that you choose from. The employer sets the menu, then the employee picks from it. They'll typically have a fixed account with a fixed rate of return, and in addition to that, some mutual funds. They'll typically offer a range of options, from conservative to aggressive investment vehicles.

Am I limited by the options the employer sets up? I can't go to my buddy who is a stockbroker and run my 401(k) through his office, right?

No, you don't have the flexibility you have on, say, an IRA, but your benefit here is that your maximum contribution limit is much higher on a 401(k). As a matter of fact, for the 1995 tax year, the contribution limit was just a tad over $9,000. Now you're not strapped down to a maximum contribution of $2,000. So you can see right there the benefit is greater tax savings in the present.

What percentage of employers contribute, versus solely the employees contributing?

That's a very difficult question to answer. Most employers who have taken the time, energy and expense to develop a 401(k) plan normally want to see it utilized and therefore motivate the employees by having a sharing arrangement. So I would say the vast majority of employers participate to some degree or another. Maybe 80%-plus of employers do, would be my guess.

And what kind of matching ratio is typical?

Typically we have seen in our practice a one-to-one matching, up to a certain point. That point normally is a maximum annual contribution that the employer would make on behalf of the employee.

For example, perhaps the employer says, "We will match up to 3% of your income." So if you're making $100,000 per year, the employer would give a maximum contribution of $3,000 in a given year.

Now realize that the employer is under no obligation to do this and anybody who has an employer that is sharing in the contribution to that 401(k) plan should be grateful. The issue is that the employer is taking money out of his pocket to take care of you in your retirement. That in fact is a very valuable benefit. Most employers use it to help build employee loyalty and to retain valuable employees.

Now realize for their contribution the employer might have what is called a 'vesting schedule.' What this means, for example, is that they say to the employee, "We're going to put this money in there for you, but if you leave our employ within the first three or four years, not all of our contribution would be yours to take with you." And they would specify a certain percentage that they would hold back until that time requirement is met. So it's not always instant growth if there's a vesting issue involved, but even when you have vesting involved, it's still a great deal for the employee.

Is a vesting schedule a fairly common thing when employers participate?

In most cases when they contribute on your behalf, that is all your money—they do not require a vesting schedule. If you leave, you take all of it with you. Only in the minority of cases is there a portion that is not yours.

There is another plan for people who work for non-profit organizations such as hospitals, schools, churches, and so forth. That is a plan called a 403(b) plan. Most teachers know about it—it is commonly called Tax Sheltered Annuities, or TSAs. Another similar form is called Tax Sheltered Custodial Accounts (TSCAs). I don't want to go into the complicated details here. This is actually very parallel to the 401(k) plan, but it is designed for people who are with non-profit organizations. Not only teachers benefit from these, but also nurses, church staff people, pastors, and so forth can take advantage of these things.

Among all of these different plans, how can I know which plan to choose?

Well I guess the very basic and most generic answer has to do with being an employer/employee or self-employed. Of course if you are an employee the plans that you have available are the ones we've already discussed, 401(k)s or 403(b)s. That's about it, and maybe you can deduct an IRA. If you are self-employed then you would look at the KEOGH plan or the SEP plan and of course you could also look at the IRA.

As you can see by all of these different types of plans, it can be quite confusing. I am of the opinion that you should talk with a qualified professional to develop the retirement plan that best suits your income objectives long-term.

Once I retire, does that mean my investment activities should cease?

That's a very good question. It really depends on your situation. In most cases people think they're going to need a substantial amount of money when they retire and then when that day arrives, they find that they're not using it all. I have several clients who say to me, "I don't want to take that money out of that IRA right now and be taxed on it. I want to continue to allow that to grow." Or, perhaps because of some astute savings or investment plan, they say, "I have money coming that I don't need and I want to reinvest it." Reinvesting earnings is a form of savings. I find that people who do plan, people who sat down some years ago and took the necessary steps to plan for their retirement, in most cases continue to reinvest some of their income.

What does 'reinvest' mean?

That means taking money—like interest or dividends—and instead of having it paid out to you, you have them pay it right back into whatever investment is producing them. That additional money, your earnings which you choose not to pocket, allows you to compound (increase) your interest—or buy additional shares of your mutual fund, for example.

What are capital gains taxes, and how do they affect my retirement income?

Capital gains taxes are the taxes that are paid on the capital gain of an investment. Let me give you an example.

Say you bought a stock for $1,000 two years ago and it has gone up to $1,500 in value and you've just sold it. The $1,000 that you originally put in is your principal. The $500 profit you made by your wise investment is called the capital gain. You pay taxes on that $500.

Currently, the top capital gains tax is 28% for investments held more than one year. You'd have to pay $140 in taxes on that gain of $500. There has been a lot of talk in Congress about reducing that tax, but as of press time for this book, it was still in effect. This money is not subject to regular income tax, but is covered by the capital gains tax.

Is there another example of a capital gain besides stock?

Certainly. You could have a capital gain on the sale of your house. But most people don't recognize it as such because the IRS allows an exception to that capital gain. If it's your principle residence, and if you buy your next home of greater value, there is no capital gains tax (as long as you do it within two years of the sale of the original house). People naturally want to move up the social ladder, or they need more room for their family, so they usually buy a home of greater value when they sell their old house.

To illustrate, say you're a young couple. You've saved the money and you bought a house for $100,000. It's not your dream house, but it is a house. Now that house has increased in value over the years to, say, $150,000. Now the $50,000 difference from what you've paid and what it is worth would theoretically be the capital gain at the time of sale. And you take that money and just roll it into a new house—let's say you pay $200,000 for that new house. The IRS has allowed you to take that $50,000 gain and roll it into a new house without having to pay the capital gains tax.

But you must have the same type of investment. Like selling a principle residence and buying a principle residence. You can't do it from a principle residence to a rental house.

But keep in mind that if you buy a new house for a lesser value than $150,000, you have to pay capital gains on the difference between the house you sold and the house you are buying (e.g., sold old house for $150,000, buying new house for $140,000, net taxable amount is $10,000).

CHAPTER 12

Tax & Estate Planning

It seems that estate planning is a fanciful notion reserved for rich people. Is that true? If not, how much money do I need to accumulate before I need to do estate planning?

I believe that if you have any assets at all, you need estate planning. Many folks consider that if you're a homeowner, that's an asset worth protecting, so folks who rent don't think it's necessary. But I go even further, since I consider my family as an asset. We all would place more value in our children than we would in our stock portfolio, or in our house, wouldn't we? To me, if you have $25 to your name and two kids, you have a need to do estate planning.

One of the greatest mistakes people make is dying without a valid will and/or some form of estate plan. You never know when this day might be your last, regardless of your age or health—thus the need is obvious for estate planning.

If you die without a valid will or other estate plan, the result is technically called 'intestacy.' That is another way of saying that the state will force its own will, or desires, upon the heirs. And it'll benefit the state for sure, you can count on that. Certainly not a good position to be in.

You mentioned 'intestacy.' Can you explain in simple terms what is involved here? How will the state and/or court system take action if I don't leave clear instructions?

They have what is called a 'static list' of how they will dispose of your estate.

What do you mean by 'static?'

That means you can't influence their process at all. If you don't have a will directing the court system, they will decide and not be obliged to listen to your desires, or those of your heirs. This includes the care of your minor children, what will happen to your house, your car(s), your boat, bank account, mutual fund account, etc. The court system will charge your estate fees because they're going to have to pay for their time and the attorneys' time, and then they're going to decide who gets the remainder of your estate after these fees are deducted from it.

Is that what is called 'probate?'

No, but probate is a part of intestacy. How's that for confusing?

Tell me about probate.

Probate occurs when you die with—or without—a valid will. When you die without a valid will, a will is created for you by the state in which you reside. Probate comes from a Latin word meaning 'to prove' and it basically says that the court will prove, or show, what you wanted to happen (even though with you dead, your true desires can't be clearly known without a valid will or estate plan). The state needs to have some kind of a process upon which to proceed, to close out your estate, and so in the absence of a plan created by you, they take action on their own. If they didn't, the courts would be backed up worse than they are now with heirs and others squabbling ad infinitum!

There are ways of eliminating probate, which we'll look at later in this chapter. Most commonly, probate is eliminated by the use of trusts. We'll look at trusts shortly.

I often see television commercials that say, "Send away today for our simple will kit, valid in all 50 states. Just $49." What do you think of offers like that? Can I write a will myself?

Do you need a will? Unequivocally, yes.

Can you write one yourself? Technically, yes. The state doesn't require an attorney to sign off on your will.

Do I recommend doing it yourself? No! I believe you should have a competent attorney do it for you. Do-it-yourself estate planning is crazy, in my opinion. Technically, you can do it yourself, but why would you want to, when a will would be relatively inexpensive—maybe $200-$300 for a simple will? Why somebody would mess around with their estate, to save a measly 200 bucks, is beyond me. You leave too much to chance that way, not knowing if it will even stand up in court. And if you're dead, you have little recourse!

Also, a will needs to be updated periodically, when laws change, or when your situation or desires change. For example, I know one family who designated another family to be guardians of their minor children, but after a few years decided they'd like someone else to do it. Unless they had changed that will, the wrong set of parents would have raised their kids!

You should review your will with your attorney at least every seven years—though annually is better. Maybe you have a new son or daughter, or new granddaughter, or grandson. Maybe your income has gone up, or gone down; maybe you've inherited some money; maybe you've saved some money. Maybe you've adopted a new child, or gotten married—or divorced. Maybe you move to a new state.

Review it even if there are no changes in your desires—the laws may have changed, or your attorney might ask you about something that hadn't occurred to you. That's why we hire professionals—to give us the edge that our own expertise doesn't cover.

How are the different laws of each state significant in my estate planning?

In some cases they can be quite different from state to state; in other ways, they are similar.

For example, California is what's called a 'community property state.' At present, there are eight community property states in the Union—which means there are 42 which aren't! Moving to, or from, a community property state can make a vast difference in how you handle your estate.

In community property states, the law holds that a married couple owns all their assets together. That is, unless specifically stated otherwise, a house, for example, would be owned by Mr. and Mrs. Jones, with them having equal rights to that property. Your will and estate plan have to be tailored to each state's treatment of this key subject.

I've heard a lot about trusts and how they can be advantageous to one's estate, yet they seem very complicated. What is a trust, anyway?

A trust is a separate legal entity that acts on behalf of the person at their death—or even during their life. It's like a corporation is, in business. Instead of the legal entity being that person, it's that person's trust.

So it's like owning your own small business: you can do business as a sole proprietor, but at a certain point you might want to incorporate.

Yes, that's a very good comparison. You act as the trustee for the trust, to make the decisions on behalf of the trust.

...just like the CEO of a corporation would make the decisions for the corporation?

Right. That's exactly the sense of a living trust.

What do I need to know about trusts?

There are very many different kinds of trusts available. Let's talk about the most common and popular one: the revocable living trust.

The key to this trust is that you have your assets titled into the trust (i.e., owned by the trust), and you act as the trustee (the person who makes the legal and binding decisions about the assets of the trust). So instead of it being John and Mary Doe, joint owners of the house, it is now The John and Mary Doe Trust as legal owner, with John and Mary Doe as the trustees. John and Mary continue to buy and sell their house, they may open bank or investment accounts, all just like normal, but instead, they do it technically through the trust. Those are the mechanics of the trust as an entity.

The big benefit of a living trust—and here you understand its popularity—is that your assets bypass the probate process at your death, which can be lengthy and costly to your estate. A trust, if titled and set up properly, guarantees staying out of probate. That way you control what happens to your assets, not some judge or attorney.

Do you eliminate the need for a will when you have a trust?

No, the will works in conjunction with the trust. The technical term for a will used with a trust is a 'pour-over will.' A pour-over will is a provision in your will that leaves all of your non-trust assets to your existing trust. It is a legal safety net. The advantage is that assets that are never held by your revocable living trust can still pass to your heirs by the provisions outlined in your trust. Note: you want to keep this amount to a minimum (i.e., under $60,000) in order to reduce the probability of non-trust assets being probated.

Once you set up a trust, is it set in concrete forevermore?

No, for the definition that we're talking about, the revocable living trust, that's a revocable and amendable document. You can amend that thing endlessly, or totally revoke the entire thing.

Is there such a thing as an irrevocable trust, where you cannot change it?

Yes, absolutely.

What are the pros and cons of the irrevocable trust?

You wouldn't want to use an irrevocable for your primary estate plan. Because your primary estate is not static, you want the ability to change your estate plan to accommodate changes in your life.

This kind of trust is just what its name implies, something that can't be revoked, or dismantled. It's for when you don't want others to be able to get their hands on your assets after you're dead. This would be used in the case of when, say, a person thinks their heirs are irresponsible and might squander their inheritance, or cheat their siblings out of their fair share of the inheritance, or something messy like that. And of course there are other reasons for using it—taxes being one.

What would be an everyday example of when I should use an irrevocable living trust, versus a revocable one?

One of the more common examples of using an irrevocable living trust is to own life insurance through the trust. Life insurance proceeds (i.e., the death benefit, money paid to the beneficiary of the insurance when the insured person dies) currently bypasses any inheritance taxes (at press time for this book, the mid-1990s). However, unfortunately the life insurance proceeds will be added into your estate for estate tax calculations, etc. if they're not owned properly. That is where an irrevocable trust could be used to act as the 'owner' of the policy, to prohibit the insurance proceeds from being taxed to the insured's estate.

Wait a minute now! I thought a death benefit was tax-free. How can it ever become taxable?

When the insurance agent says that the death benefit is tax-free, in fact, he is correct. To the beneficiary, it is tax-free. But that's not the whole picture. Let me illustrate.

Let's say Mom and Dad both die in a car wreck and the kids are the life insurance beneficiaries. The kids say, "Okay, it's bad that our parents died, but it's great in that we get a half-million dollars' worth of life insurance and we don't have to pay any taxes on it." That's technically correct. But now the federal government says, "Wait a minute—Dad owned that life insurance, it is part of his estate, and therefore we're going to include that in the estate when we figure federal estate taxes." So they add that $500,000 into the total of his estate to use as a factor in figuring out the federal estate taxes.

So even though the money—the death benefit—goes to the kids, the government counts that against the dead parents in figuring out the estate taxes? That does-

n't seem fair.

Unfortunately it isn't fair, but that's the way government regulations can be sometimes. If you have an irrevocable life insurance trust own Dad's policy, you prevent the death benefits from being included in Dad and Mom's estate. That is the solution to that scenario we just looked at. The irrevocable trust owns the life insurance policy instead of Mom and Dad. The kids are still the beneficiaries, but the trust is a separate legal entity from Mom and Dad. Therefore you prevent the life insurance proceeds from being a taxable asset for the federal estate taxes, which are typically very high—starting at 37% and going to 55%.

What are the other kinds of trusts besides the ones you have mentioned?

There are an awful lot of trusts out there, but the other one that I think deserves some attention is called a charitable remainder trust.

This is a trust that is used to eliminate, in many cases, a capital gains tax on a highly appreciated investment. To illustrate, let's say you bought a home in the 1960s at $10,000 and now it is worth $400,000. If you sold that home, you'd have a horrendous capital gains tax to pay. Let's say it was a rental property and you don't intend on living in it (i.e., the principal residence exemption we discussed in chapter 11 would not apply). So you are effectively prevented from selling it because you'd lose probably one-third of its value to capital gains tax. So you hold on to it.

What can you do? You can put this house in a trust, a charitable remainder trust, so the trust—not you—can now sell the home and not have to pay capital gains tax. The proceeds of that sale are held in trust for your use. You could have the full value of that home, $400,000, invested and be taking the income it produces and avoid that nasty capital gains tax.

In simple terms if you did not do this trust arrangement, and were to sell it and pay the capital gains tax, you would probably only have about $268,000 left to invest after you sold it. Say you were able to get an 8% income from that—that'd give you about $21,500 a year in income. Whereas if you put the asset in the trust, and have the charitable trust sell the asset, you would have the full $400,000 that could be invested. At 8%, you would have about $32,000 a year income, or about $10,500 more income each year than if you had not used the trust. That's a significant difference.

Plus, there are some other benefits of the charitable remainder trust.

Not only do you eliminate the capital gains tax paid on that sale, but you also receive a charitable tax deduction (of $400,000 in our example) in the year that you establish the trust and put that property in the trust.

Why does the IRS give you that charitable tax deduction?

Because ultimately, upon the death of the surviving spouse (let's say it is a husband and wife who did this trust), that designated charity would get the remainder of the assets. So even though you've 'given the house to charity' in a sense, while you're still alive you can receive the income that the bundle of money ($400,000) produces, even though the principal is reserved for the eventual ownership of the charity.

And when you're gone, the remainder then goes to the charity. But before you die, that bundle of money can do work for you, by earning interest, or yield from investments. (Of course, you have to pay income tax on the earnings, as normal. But the principal is untouched by the tax man.) It's really a nifty win-win for both the individual *and* the charity.

I see, so this is a way to give your house to charity—eventually—but along the way to enjoy some income—right?

Yes. You not only get to be nice to your favorite charity, but also earn money the donation can earn now, while you're alive. The idea here is that you get some substantial tax benefits while you're still living and while you need them. And the charity, even though it can't use the money while you're alive, can still know that they will have that money someday, and plan on it. Plus, you can have the flexibility of changing the charity before you die, and the basic arrangement (as far as it concerns the IRS) still remains the same.

You say the charity receives the remainder—does that imply that there might not be $400,000 left when you die?

That is correct. But it can go both ways. It might have grown or it might have shrunk. In this case, the real estate market might have tanked. So the term 'remainder' doesn't necessarily mean less; rather, it refers to that which 'remains' after your death.

Let's say in my example that we're going to try to establish an 8% income from this trust, but let's say that over the years we average better than that: we averaged 10%. That often happens. So it might be giving the charity _more_ than $400,000 at the end.

Another benefit is the fact that by putting it in a trust you don't have that asset being subject to federal estate taxes, like the life insurance example we just looked at. So depending on your situation, that could be a very big benefit to your heirs.

So the charitable remainder trust is a savvy way for folks to leave some assets to a charity at their death but make it work for them while they are still alive. In my view, there's no reason to give a huge chunk of assets to Uncle Sam. I say, let Uncle Sam spend his money wisely and rely on normal taxes, like income taxes.

What would be a typical cost to set up such a trust?

Most of the attorneys I have talked with charge anywhere from $800-$1,200 to establish a simple trust, so it is not very costly—especially in comparison to the financial benefits you receive.

How does my death affect my IRA account, and my other investments?

That's a very good question. With an IRA you have a named beneficiary. In our simple example of a husband and wife, let's say the husband owns the IRA and the wife is the beneficiary. There is a rule that says you should always have a backup beneficiary. So perhaps you would have your children as a secondary beneficiary if something happens to you and your wife simultaneously.

Often when people come in to set up the trust they'll ask me, "Should I name my trust as a primary beneficiary of my IRA?" I usually say they should _not_ name the trust as the primary beneficiary, but they could name it as the secondary beneficiary.

You would normally have your spouse as the primary beneficiary because the spouse has the opportunity to roll those IRA funds into his own IRA and not have to pay tax on any of that income in the year that the spouse passed away. On the other hand, if you name the trust as the primary beneficiary, then in the year that either spouse died, you would have to pay tax on the full amount of the IRA—which would be very costly, and in most cases unnecessary. The one thing the IRS does allow is surviving spouses to roll over the deceased spouse's IRA into their own—that way they are able to retain the tax-deferred growth of their retirement savings.

Do you often see this error occurring—that of people naming their trust as the beneficiary of the IRA?

Quite frequently, yes. People think, *I'm changing the title on all my other assets to go to the trust, so why not my IRA?* And many do, unless their attorney or financial advisor explains in detail why they should not.

How can I minimize the tax bite on my estate?

This is a critical question of supreme importance. Again, I'm all for paying our fair share of taxes, but let's not be stupid about it! Let's work within the law to minimize the amount of taxes we much pay.

Let's first establish how much we get to pass on to our heirs tax-free. The IRS allows every U.S. citizen to pass on to his heirs $600,000 free of estate tax. So if you have an estate of $600,000 or less, you don't have to be concerned about an estate tax bite at all. This applies to individuals, not couples—so if a dead father leaves his estate to his son and daughter-in-law, he gets $600,000 and she gets $600,000.

Now let's talk about if you have more than $600,000 in assets in your estate when you die. Let's say John and Mary Doe have a combined estate worth, say, $1 million. Under a simple analysis, you'd say, "Well, $1 million divided by two is $500,000 for each spouse," and it looks like we've done our job—i.e, that neither has more than $600,000. But what happens most commonly is that the husband and wife each leave the remaining estate to what we call 'either/or.' In essence, the husband says, "If I die, everything goes to my wife," and the wife says, "If I die, everything goes to my husband." Sounds good, doesn't it? Nice and simple.

But in reality, tax-wise, it's not good.

Let's say the husband dies first. Now Mary's estate is worth $1 million, not $500,000, because John left all his money to her. Next, a few years later, Mary dies and her estate may now be properly taxed on the basis of $1 million. That's $400,000 more than the $600,000 exemption she gets from the IRS. Therefore she has a federal estate tax of about $150,000 (about 38% of that $400,000 overage). Ouch!

Because John and Mary didn't do their estate planning, they now have created a situation that is irreversible—they just turned her taxable estate from $500,000 into $1 million—and that is a big problem. The deceased husband never got to use his $600,000 exemption.

The obvious question is: How do we solve that? We go back to our toolbox of trusts. In this case we would use a form of revocable living trust that is called commonly known as a bypass trust. We create two trusts: one for John, and one for Mary. We park $500,000 in each, since they are worth $1 million in this example. Then when John passes away, his $500,000 is 'safe' from estate taxes, and Mary doesn't all of a sudden become worth $1 million, exposing herself to taxes above the exemption limit. This allows the husband to utilize his credit of up to $600,000 and keep the integrity of his side of the estate intact and tax-free, and the wife is able to use her $600,000 exemption, too. Thus the children, if they are the ultimate beneficiaries, would receive the full $1 million, and not have to give the IRS that $150,000 estate tax bite.

One further issue to keep in mind is what I said earlier about some states that are community property states and some that are not. How you handle the titling of assets in each state in some cases can be a little bit different. That is why you need to consult with a qualified financial advisor. It's too detailed to explain it all here. Get with an attorney who does trusts in your state and you'll be set up okay.

There is one common mistake that I see often in my practice which bears mention here. It commonly occurs when you have, say, a widow who has two children and she owns a house. She then puts the two children on the title as owners, listed as joint tenants. She incorrectly thinks that she is helping her son or daughter by putting the title of that property in his or her name. She knows she wants to give the house to them eventually, after her death, so why not do it now, in terms of the titling? She feels that if anything happened to her, it'd be better for them to have title, so they could sell the house if she went into a nursing facility, or that they could borrow against it if there were, say, huge medical bills involved with her care.

By listing them as joint tenants, she may think that such a setup will bypass probate, and in a technical sense that's true. She thinks, *Gee, I don't want to have my kids subject to probate, so by doing it this way I'm being smart and making it easier on them.*

But in reality this causes a great deal of mess when Mom passes away. There are many inherent problems with this setup—too many to list here. Suffice to say, you need to talk to an experienced estate advisor in your state before making that kind of decision. It doesn't even matter whether your state is a community property state, or not—in most cases, both types of jurisdiction view this as messy.

How do I best handle lump-sum distributions, such as a pension paying out, or an inheritance I receive?

If you are the surviving spouse and receive a pension plan or an IRA plan from your deceased partner, you'd want to roll it into your own IRA so you don't have to pay the tax. The only exception to that is, if you are not the surviving spouse, but rather you are one of the children of the spouses. In that case, you would be responsible to pay the taxes on the pension amount that you would receive. That's because the tax-deferred roll-over provision of the pension or IRA is only available to a surviving spouse.

If it is an inheritance, it's different, since in many cases you don't have to be concerned about taxes because the estate of the deceased will already have paid estate taxes before you get the money. You are therefore not obligated to pay income taxes on an inheritance.

What role should life insurance play in estate planning?

There are two purposes for life insurance: one is to create an estate and the other is to preserve an estate. When I say create an estate, that is to provide for your family. In a simple example, you have a married couple with two children; if the breadwinner were to die, there would need to be enough money to raise the children, educate them, and take care of the surviving spouse. That is the first case where you need life insurance.

The other case is when you have done a good job at financial planning, you've created a reasonable amount of wealth and now you've got an estate tax bill staring you in the face at the death of you and your spouse. In that case what you want to do is have enough life insurance to pay for the estate taxes so that you can pass your entire estate on to your children or your heirs.

Can you tell me about the various kinds of life insurance, briefly, with pros and cons of each?

Well, number one, term insurance is designed to provide a death benefit only—there is no other purpose for it. You pay a premium and at the death of the insured, the benefit is received by the beneficiary. Very simple. You're not putting money in to save or accumulate 'cash values.' The pro of term insurance is it is normally inexpensive—especially when you're younger (i.e., less than 50 years old). The downside is that as you get older, it can get very expensive—in some cases so expensive you can't afford it. I guess that is a worst-case scenario; if you became uninsurable because you have cancer or a heart problem, you might not be able to renew your term insurance and that could be catastrophic.

The second kind of insurance is called 'whole life' insurance. This contract allows a cash savings or buildup, along with the death benefit. The benefits of whole life is that the premium amount is fixed for your whole life—thereby its name. Its downside is that it is usually a higher monthly premium, and in some cases the 'cash value' does not build up very quickly. This is because some of the premium is used to go into cash savings for the insured, and some is used to pay the sales commission and overhead of the insurer, and what's left is used to buy the insurance itself—that is, the death benefit.

Some critics of whole life have said that it is a poor investment option because the cash value within whole life does not earn extremely high interest rates, as opposed to commonly available other investment options. Its opponents say you are better off buying term insurance than whole life insurance, and investing the difference between what the two forms cost. There are some risks in doing that, so be sure to do your homework.

The third type of insurance is called 'universal life.' It is very similar to whole life in that you have a premium that pays for the insurance and adds to the cash value, but the premium isn't fixed like whole life and the cash value interest can vary. This is somewhat complex, and I don't want to go into all the details here. You need to talk with a qualified financial planner or insurance agent with regard to universal life insurance.

The fourth and final type of insurance is called 'variable universal life.' This allows you to choose from a menu of different mutual fund accounts where you want the cash value invested. So this gives you more flexibility as far as your being able to direct how and where your premium dollars are invested. But the premium and rate of return aren't fixed and the performance of the investments is predicated on the performance of the funds within the policy that you choose. So there is potentially a greater risk in this form versus other forms of insurance.

The beauty of variable universal life is that you can influence the cash value by the type of investments you choose. The downside is that if your investments do poorly, you might not have as much cash value as you would have otherwise through traditional insurance contracts.

CHAPTER 13

Speculative Investments

What types of investments are considered speculative?

Speculative investments are any investment in which you are betting on, or anticipating, an extraordinarily high rate of return, and which carry a huge rate of risk. They might include investments in which there are many unpredictable factors (more than the usual amount of forecasting, exceeding the rise and fall of stock market prices), such as weather, acts of God, etc.

In the case of wheat futures, for example (a form of commodities trading which we'll examine in this chapter), if Kansas suffers a huge hailstorm just before harvest time, that's going to destroy a large part of the wheat crop, and affect the price severely. There's an example of the unpredictability of these types of investments. Put another way, you can attempt to analyze the rise or fall of, say, GM stock, but predicting the weather six months in advance is really getting out on the proverbial limb.

There are four types of speculative investments I want to talk about in this chapter. Number one is futures contracts; two is commodities futures; three is interest rate futures; four is stock index futures.

First of all, let's talk about why futures were established. They are really meant for the agricultural community, so that farmers could sell their product before they got to market. Let's say it's April and that I am raising corn, and I don't know what the price of corn is going to be at harvest time, in the fall. I don't even know if God is going to wipe out my crop through a drought or a flood or whatever. I can either do it the traditional way and plant my crop, wait until harvest time and then take whatever the market price is at that time, or I can participate in the futures market. This is a way to get my money in advance, or at least to know what my income is going to be in advance.

So in the futures agreement, I say, "Okay, I will agree on a price for my corn in advance." I give a contract to an investor who says, "I will pay you a dollar a bushel for your corn." The investor then takes the risk of whether it is going to be wiped out (e.g., drought hits and he loses all his money) or whether it is going to bring a price of $1.50 a bushel, in which case he makes a profit. Or it brings a price of $.90 a bushel, in which case he loses money.

The farmer gets paid the buck per bushel, and at least gets his money up front. He may not be rolling in cash, but he's safe, in that at least he's been paid. Let's say the price goes to $1.50/bushel by harvest time—if the investor can sell his contract and get paid $1.50 he gets ahead for risking his capital during the growing season. And he helps the farmer out by acting as a hedge against the crop being lost to, say, a natural disaster like a flood.

The futures market has developed quite a bit over the years. A market has been created to buy these contracts on open exchanges, just like you buy stocks and bonds in New York. There are futures exchanges around the country, like the CBOT (Chicago Board of Trade) where they buy and sell commodities futures and trade in futures and other option contracts. The general public can thus gamble on the future price of any commodity, like soy beans, rice, wheat, or pork bellies. What's more, most of the buyers never actually take delivery of that corn or wheat. They sell the contract they made with the farmer at some point in time, they cash it out. Especially if the 'going rate' is going up, they will sell so they can profit. Or if it is going down, they'll sell so they can limit their loss.

So the futures market is just like the stock market. For every buyer there is a seller.

Doesn't the eventual person who is left holding that option at harvest time take delivery?

When the contract matures (e.g., that commodity is harvested), the investor sells the corn, say, at the market price at that time. They don't actually take delivery; it just goes to the granary and then their check is delivered.

What is the commodities market all about?

What the commodities market does is extend the futures market in the sense that contracts are between individuals that really have no interest in those commodities. Traders don't care if the corn is sweet, or abundant, or scarce; they only care about the profit they can make from buying at one price and selling at another. (Now if the abundance or scarcity affects the price—and it usually does—*then* they care! That's capitalism at work.) Or, they may bet on the price of copper, or aluminum, or gold—anything that has an intrinsic value to it. What they are essentially doing is betting on the rise and fall in prices.

How are commodities related to 'options?'

Commodities *are* options; they are part of the options market. You buy an option, counting on the eventuality that the commodity is going to rise in price.

Under the options market, you would have stock options that you can write contracts on the rise and fall of the prices of stock. Instead of actually owning the stock, you are simply taking a contract on the basis of whether it is going to rise or fall in price.

Do financial advisors oftentimes use the term 'options' and 'futures' interchangeably?

Yes, they do. There is only a subtle difference between the two terms. They share a lot in common—the common denominator being this betting aspect about predicting future prices.

Should I buy options and/or commodities as a part of my investment strategy?

Average investors shouldn't get themselves involved with the options market, because it is very complicated and extremely risky. My advice to everybody reading this book is that if you get a call from a broker who says he can make you a ton of money in the futures market, hang up. Let the people who are caught up in the world of speculation do those things. One of the things that happens to people who speculate is that they can get addicted to this kind of a market, just like an alcoholic is addicted to booze.

Why is that?

It's a form of gambling, and gamblers get a thrill from that type of action. It is the greed factor that is involved in trying to make a quick buck and finding the pot at the end of the rainbow. That is what drives these types of personalities—they feed on the excitement of making a pile of dough quickly, and with little effort.

For instance, I have a client in Florida who got a call a few years ago from a broker. The investor had no understanding whatsoever about what he was doing by agreeing to do what the broker suggested. Because of the promise by the broker that it was 'a sure thing' that he could profit, making 50-300% in profit, the man put most of his savings into it—and lost every dime within just a few weeks. You have to remember that the only thing the commodities broker is interested in is the huge commission that is charged to your account.

What is a typical commission for these types of transactions?

Well, it can run up to 10-15% of the money you invest. So you have to remember that. It's higher than traditional stockbrokerage commissions. It is a very quick sell, it is a very quick 'in' and a very quick 'out.' That is, commodities brokers can make more money on fewer transactions, or sales, than stockbrokers. So you have to beware of get-rich-quick brokers, too.

Does your firm deal in commodities, futures, options, in your portfolio management services for your clients?

Even though I am licensed to do options, futures, commodities, I don't allow them to be bought for any client of ours. They are prohibited investments in my office.

A lot of people ask me if these speculative types of investments are a borderline form of gambling. Well, they are not borderline gambling; they are full-bore gambling. It can get ugly; what happens to such a man who loses money in this market is that he is always looking for ways to make it back. So he gets caught in a hamster wheel where he is trying to recoup his losses at all times. He believes that sooner or later he is going to strike it rich. He's like a guy throwing quarters into a slot machine in Las Vegas. He throws in three dollars and he gets back $3,000, and now he's hooked. He's got a bucket full of coins and he thinks that he can increase it by 1,000 times again. Before you know it, he's down $300, so he just keeps pulling the lever on the slot machine. Once he gets the taste of making money this way, he often can't stop. The 'one-armed bandit' strikes again. That is exactly what happens on these trading markets.

Have any of your clients gotten burned in this area?

Yes, we have a client who is addicted to the futures market. It has been very difficult for him to manage his money. We have had to tie up certain amounts of the money in good quality investments in order to keep him from spending the rest of his money on the futures markets.

Does he feel better now that he's got a financial advisor to help him steer his ship, so to speak? How's he doing?

Because of my more conservative posture, he takes his long-term money and puts it in the vehicles we recommend. But to accommodate his desires (after all, he's the client; it's his money) to play the markets, we have separated his money into two parts—some we manage, some he manages. There is still a certain amount of money that I have not been able to get away from him that he still spends on these risky investments.

So he still does it because he likes it, but in other words, the quantities are not such that it is going to ruin his estate?

That is correct. We've limited his losses. Again, I do not allow any of the financial advisors working for me to recommend futures transactions; that's not to say that clients like this particular one won't decide on their own to use their assets in this way.

Should I have any of my portfolio in speculative investments?

No. You should keep your portfolio as conservative and as safe as you can at all times, while still making the best yield possible with reasonable risk. I believe that is just a prudent way to handle money. The C-SIS method encourages such a balance.

What does the term 'direct investment' mean?

This would mean an investment in which we don't have an exchange where we trade investments, such as the NYSE. We buy shares of a company or a project directly from the company itself. Direct investments are commonly bought in 'units' instead of shares.

I will give you a couple of examples. There are a few great investments that I use frequently with my clients. One is Jones Cable, or Jones Intercable, which I believe is about the fifth-largest cable TV company in the United States. Jones derives a lot of its money directly from the public, in direct investments. If they want to build a cable system somewhere, say in Chicago or Los Angeles, or in England, they ask the brokers to raise money from their client base to finance their project. The return comes from the fact that the cable system would be sold at a future date and the profit would be shared with the investors, depending on how many units each investor owned.

Some companies, like Jones Cable and others, have another program where they pay a stated return of interest on the money invested with them. They pay that either monthly or quarterly. These programs are commonly known as limited partnerships. There are good ones and there are bad ones. We covered limited partnerships earlier in the book, when we looked at oceangoing container leasing, and triple-net leasing of commercial buildings.

Another type of deal we've found to be solid is where a company leases equipment, like big Caterpillar earth-moving equipment, or a fleet of trucks, things like that.

Are direct investments considered speculative?

Yes, they are, because direct investments have higher than average degrees of risk. That simply means you have to be very sure of your information before you invest. For example, I myself did the research firsthand on Jones Cable. I was confident that they were a solid investment, and it has paid off nicely for us.

In contrast, oil and gas leasing is one of the riskiest things you can get into, as we've seen. In the mid-'90s, Prudential Securities, Inc. had to settle a lawsuit involving nearly $750 million, brought by more than 99,000 investors, because their limited partnerships went sour, and the investors charged that Prudential had defrauded them. So many of those have gone sour that investors are very afraid of limited partnerships, even though some great ones exist, if you know how to assess and buy them.

What are typical costs, including both the buy-in cost and also sales commissions, for limited partnerships?

Most partnerships have a $5,000 minimum per investor. Units typically run $500 to $1,000 per unit ($500 is more common). Typically you might buy 10 units at $500 each to hit the minimum of $5,000 per investor. Or you could buy 1,000 units at $500 each, a total investment of $500,000.

What about commissions?

Commissions paid on limited partnerships are typically between 5-8%.

Are direct investments things that investors can do by themselves?

No. Direct investments require an investment advisor or broker to be involved.

Why is that?

That's the government's way of protecting the investor from being ripped off through buying things they don't understand, especially in this arena. So that is why the brokerage houses are required to do their due diligence, so the investor has at least a fighting chance to know that this investment is a good one.

So there are government regulations governing this type of investment?

Certainly. Those investments have to be registered in their respective states, as well as with the United States government. And a prospectus (brochure) is required to be sent out explaining the investment

There is a secondary market (where you could sell your units after you bought them to other investors) for these, but it is very, very small. So a person buying a direct investment must keep in mind that if he is going to cash out early, he would probably only get up to 50% of what he paid, if sold any time before maturity. That's due to the higher than normal risk factor, and also to the illiquidity of these things. So you had better believe in the direct investment itself if you invest in it; wait out the term and hope you get a share of the profits. It's not like the bond market or options market in that sense. The main thing about direct investments for the investor to remember is that they are illiquid. When you're in, you're in—and you cannot get out without losing your shirt.

What is the typical time frame on direct investments?

Usually six to 10 years. Some will run up to 14 years or longer.

What is a typical yield for direct investments?

A lot of them pay very well. There have been some direct investments that have paid six to eight times the original investment value. Even given the fact that you must wait seven years, that's still about 100% per year. You can't get that just anywhere.

Then there are some that pay a stated rate of return—say, an income stream of 10% per annum. I have one investment that I use that is a direct investment that pays 10% per annum, paid every month—and for 20-plus years it has never missed a payment to the investor.

Are those fairly rare among direct investments?

They are not rare with us, because I have guidelines we use. We will not buy any kind of direct investment that is leveraged, for example.

What does that mean?

'Leverage' means that they borrowed the money to pay for their enterprise. So if it is paid for 100% in cash and they have no debt, then the investment may very well be fairly safe, assuming all the other factors are in place. Some direct investments have set themselves up so they cannot have any debt—by the company's own rules, and they register with the government that way. The key is to find those kinds of companies that are on solid financial ground.

Plus, read the prospectus! Because in the little-bitty print of the prospectus you might miss something key. So spend the time to research these things, even as the investor. Sure, your financial advisor is there to advise you, but check up on him by reading all of your contracts and advisory documents. Sure, the language may be difficult to decipher, but ask questions and understand it all before taking the plunge.

You don't always make money in direct investments. Sometimes that's not the goal of the investor—sometimes he wants to _lose_ money! An advantage here is the pass-through of losses to the investor. In the case of limited partnerships, the general partner (i.e., the company running the enterprise) can take part of its expenses in the first two or three years and pass through those expenses to the limited partner (i.e., the investor), who can take a portion of that off his taxes. Sometimes a loss can be handy for some investors at tax time; it reduces their taxes.

What other types of exotic investments are available in direct investments?

Exotic is a good word because these investments are indeed exotic and the public knows very little about them. Let me give you one. There is a limited partnership/direct investment that is designed to lose 100% of your money. Let's say you put $100,000 into a real estate program. The partners buy the poorest, most dilapidated properties they possibly can, in slum areas often, knowing that the renters in the slum areas are going to default on their rent payments and that the project will never be profitable.

So what happens is that you put $100,000 in it and your balance is designed to be $0 in 10 years. The advantage of that is that the investor who needs a tax write-off takes every dime of that loss directly off his taxes. Not only in the year of its occurrence, but also he pro-rates that loss year by year, portioning a part of that huge loss for many years on his taxes. And it's all perfectly legal. You can invest in anything that loses money. The IRS says in effect, "If you're stupid enough to do that, it's fine with us."

Should I invest in gold or silver?

Well, that's a big debate out there in investor-land, but the way I see it, it's pretty simple. My personal opinion is that you should *never* have in your portfolio more than a 5% position in gold, silver, or precious metals.

From the long-term standpoint, gold is relatively unattractive. First of all, it has no income; it just sits there. There is no return in excess of the inflation rate, generally. If you looked at the gold in Britain over the last 400 years, its rate of return has only been one-tenth of 1%. That's pretty poor. On this side of the pond, if you've looked at inflation in the United States of 1.7% to 7%, from 1926 to 1992, then gold makes no sense at all. Only if it makes the investor feel better does it make sense to invest in gold.

Isn't that what gold enthusiasts say—that gold is an enduring commodity? Does it add stability?

Well, it can add stability. For instance, if we were to have a huge crash and a big fiasco, an Armageddon in our economy, then certainly gold is going to have value, and people who have it stored are going to bring it out, and it might eventually become the fixed standard in a chaotic setting. If you believe that is going to happen, I would say you should put everything you have in gold.

But if you don't believe it's going to happen—and I don't—then you would be foolish to buy too much gold. For instance, what's the price of gold right now? At press time, gold was $360 per ounce. What was the price in 1980? The same: $360 per ounce. Yes, it went up to $700 briefly in the early 1990s and people bought it, but then it went right back down to $360, so what happened to those people who bought it at $700? They will never recoup their losses, it seems. So, to me it makes no sense in our market, in our world today, to buy gold.

Some people feel that the United States should go back to the gold standard as a basis for our currency. What is your advice on that—should we go back to the gold standard as a basis for our currency?

No, we should not, because if we do, we cannot control inflation. We cannot control the money supply with a fixed commodity backing our currency. The current system, managed by the Fed, is the best system possible.

Here is something that people are unaware of. The United States was on a gold standard from 1868 to 1971, when Nixon took us off it. But even then, only 25% of our currency was backed by gold. So it is a misconception that there are a 'bizillion' ounces of gold at Fort Knox, and that we should just standardize our whole currency on that supply of yellow metal. We cannot, even if we wanted to.

So it's really a false hope.

It's a false hope, and it's a silly hope for anybody to say that. It's never going to happen in this country.

Have other countries based their currencies on precious metals and has it worked for them?

In the past they have, but in the free market economies that have emerged in modern times, such as Germany, France, and England, the answer is no. They operate on fiat money, or a credit system, just like we do. Some countries still have a small amount of their currency backed by gold, but those countries have a horrible time controlling inflation.

Is Russia a good example of that?

Russia is a great example. Their economy is in a chaotic mess today.

If you take the advice of a doomsayer who tells you that we ought to be back on the gold standard, here is what's going to happen. Russia at some point in time is going to standardize the ruble. They have to. They haven't yet because they're not in a position to, and that's a whole other story, but when they do, they are going to flood the world market with gold. They own half of the world's gold supply. So what is going to happen to the price of gold? It could be $55 per ounce, down from $360. Investors would be destitute if they put all of their eggs in that golden basket.

I recently debated Bill Dannemeyer over national radio on the subject of the gold standard. He's a former U.S. Congressman from Orange County, California. A caller phoned in and asked how much of her portfolio should be in gold. He said you shouldn't have more than 10%. Even being a non-investment advisor, he knew not to load up on gold. But he never expounded as to why. And the reason is, as every bona fide financial advisor will tell you, it is not a prudent move by the United States government to fix our currency on a commodity. It would devastate this economy.

What is the future of the gold and silver market?

I think it is going to be in the future just what it has been in the past. People who are 'gold bugs' are going to keep screaming that doomsday is coming, and we ought to buy gold. Mostly they are the pessimistic-type doomsayers that want to load up with water and food in their basements for the great Armageddon. And they put some gold down there too, just for good measure!

There is a book that we discovered, written by one of the leading doomsayers in our country, Larry Burkett, that was written back in the early 1980s, entitled *Surviving the Underground Economy*. In that book, he predicted that there were going to be these marauding gangs that were going to raid your pantry and generally mess up your life in the economic chaos he believes is coming. When was the last time you or your friends had marauding gangs bother your neighborhood? Sure, some of the inner cities are not nice at night, but this is not a common phenomenon throughout our great land.

I still find it hard to believe that such a high percentage of the content of that book is so consistently fallacious. The whole premise is that the entire world is going to fall apart—and soon. It is like Chicken Little in the old fairy tale, running around crying, "The sky is falling! The sky is falling!" If you are going to adhere to that kind of philosophy, you are going to get beat up investment-wise, and a lot of other people are, too.

When I wrote my *Exploding the Doomsday Money Myths* book, virtually 100% of the financial advisors who called me from around the country were saying, 'It's about time somebody set all of this doomsday stuff straight.'

Here is what I believe. I still trust in America. I trust in her resilience, her entrepreneurship, and everything else that has made her great. And as emerging markets open up worldwide, the third world world will become the new American West for our growing economy, and indeed for the global marketplace to grow in.

As far as investments go, no matter what the future holds, I want to be in a position that is rock-solid, and that why I'm promoting the C-SIS method. Hiding gold in my basement, or burying it in my backyard, is utter foolishness.

EPILOGUE

  This book is not intended to upend any financial strategy a person may now be using—i.e., you should not rush right out and fire your stockbroker and go with a totally fee-based management system, or vice versa. Rather, it is to be used as a guide to help educate you about investment alternatives.

  It is written to educate and inform the neophyte investor, so he can better understand how the investment world impacts all our lives. It is meant as a primer about how investments work, without delving into extensive education. And it is designed to help the investor understand more clearly exactly what his investment advisor is doing with his funds, in order to keep him informed as a consumer of financial services.

  Every day, on almost every television and radio channel, there are stock reports. Our newspapers and magazines carry the entire New York Stock Exchange reports daily, plus many of the mutual funds. Millions of people wonder as they listen to the radio during those stock market reports just what this is all about. This book was written to help you understand a little bit better what is going on out there—and how you can take advantage of it personally.

  I understand how difficult it is to read investment books. I have read plenty, and, before I received my in-depth education on the subject, I had the same difficulty most everyone has, in deciphering all the financial jargon. My hope is that each reader has found this book not only interesting, but has learned much from it as well.

Planning for our financial futures is extremely important in the society in which we live and work. If this book has made the way easier, then I have successfully done my job.

APPENDIX:

A Glossary of
Financial & Investment Terms

A

Accrued Interest. Interest that has accrued on a bond since the payment of the last coupon. The purchaser of a bond pays the accrued interest plus the market price.

B

Bear Market. A period of time (usually months) during which measures of the stock market decline.

Bid Price. The price at which the specialist or dealer offers to buy shares.

Blue-Chip Stocks. Stocks of the highest quality, with long records of earnings and dividends—well known, stable, mature companies.

Bond. Long-term debt instrument representing a contractual obligation on the part of the issuer to pay interest and repay principal.

Bond Ratings. Letters (e.g., AAA, AA, etc.) assigned to bonds to express their relative probability of default. Widely recognized ratings are done by Standard & Poor's and Moody's.

Bond Swaps. An active bond management strategy involving the purchase and sale of bonds in an attempt to improve the rate of return on the bond portfolio. There are several different types of bond swaps.

Book Value. The value of a corporation's equity as shown on the books (i.e., the balance sheet).

Broker. An intermediary who represents buyers or sellers in securities transactions and receives a commission. The broker acts in the best interest of the customer.

Bull Market. A period of time (usually months) during which measures of the stock market rise.

Business Cycle. Reflects movements in aggregate economic activity.

Business Risk. The risk of a company suffering losses, or profits less than expected, for some time period because of adverse circumstances in the company's particular line of activity.

C

Call. An option to buy stock at a stated price within a specified period of nine months or less.

Capital Gain. The amount by which the sale price of a security exceeds the purchase price.

Capital Loss. The amount by which the sale price of a capital asset is less than its purchase price.

Capital Market. The market for long-term securities such as bonds and stocks.

Cash Account. The most common type of brokerage account in which a customer may make only cash transactions.

Certificates of Deposit. (1) If negotiable, a marketable short-term deposit liability of the issuer that pays principal (minimum of $100,000) plus interest at maturity; (2) if non-negotiable, savings certificates with varying maturities and interest rates.

Convertible Securities. Bonds or preferred stock that are convertible, at the holder's option, into shares of common stock of the same corporation.

Corporate Bonds. Long-term debt securities of various types sold by corporations.

Coupon Bond. Coupon refers to the periodic interest payments paid by the issuer to the bondholders. Most bonds are coupon bonds.

Current Yield. The yield on a security resulting from dividing the interest payment or dividend by the current market price.

Cyclical Industries. Industries that usually do well when the economy prospers and are likely to be hurt when it falters.

D

Dealer. And individual (firm) who buys and sells securities for his or her own account. Dealers in OTC (over the counter) securities profit by the spread between the bid and ask prices.

Debenture. An unsecured bond, backed by the general credit of a company.

Defensive Industries. Industries least affected by recessions and economic adversity.

Discount Broker. Brokerage firms offering execution services at prices typically less than full-line brokerage firms.

Dividends. The only cash payments regularly made by corporations to their stockholders.

Dow Jones Industrial Average (DJIA). A price-weighted series of 30 leading industrial stocks, used as measure of stock market activity.

E

E/P Ratio. A capitalization rate used to capitalize earnings—the reciprocal or the P/E ratio.

Ex Ante. Before the fact—what is expected to occur.

Expected Return. The ex ante return expected by investors over some future holding period. The expected return often differs from the realized return.

F

Federal Agency Securities. Securities issued by the federal credit agencies. Federal agency securities are fully guaranteed, whereas government-sponsored agency securities are not.

Financial Risk. Risk arising from the use of debt in financing the assets of a firm.

Financial Statements. The major financial data provided by a corporation, primarily the balance sheet and the income statement.

Fixed-Income Securities. Securities with specified payment dates and amounts, primarily bonds and preferred stock.

Fundamental Analysis. The idea that a security has an intrinsic value at any time which is a function of underlying economic variables. By analyzing these variables, intrinsic value can be estimated.

Futures Contracts. Agreements providing for the future exchange of a particular asset at a currently determined market price.

G
Generally Accepted Accounting Principles (GAAPs). A standard set of rules developed by the accounting profession for the preparation of financial statements.

H
None.

I
Index Funds. Mutual funds holding portfolios that attempt to duplicate a market average, such as the S&P 500.

Indirect Investing. The buying and selling of the shares of investment companies which, in turn, hold portfolios of securities. This is an investor alternative to direct investing.

Individual Retirement Accounts (IRAs). Tax-sheltered accounts available to all income earners. IRA funds can be invested in a wide range of assets.

Institutional Investors. Pension funds, investment companies, bank trust departments, life insurance companies, and so forth, all of whom manage large portfolios of securities.

Interest Rate Futures. Futures contracts on fixed-income securities such as treasury bills and bonds, CDs, and GNMA mortgages.

Interest Rate Options. Option contracts on fixed-income securities such as treasury bonds.

Interest Rate Risk. The change in the price of a security resulting from a change in market interest rates.

Intrinsic Value. The economic value of an asset.

Investment. The commitment of funds to one or more assets that will be held over some future time period.

Investment Bankers. Firms specializing in the sale of new securities to the pubic, typically by underwriting the issue.

J
Junk Bond. Bonds that carry ratings of BB or lower, with correspondingly higher yields. The junk bond market is perhaps better referred to as the 'high-yield debt market.'

K
None.

L

Leverage. The magnification of gains and losses in earnings resulting from the use of fixed-cost financing.

Limit Order. An order to buy or sell at a specified (or better) price.

Liquidity. The ease with which an asset can be bought or sold quickly with relatively small price changes.

Load Funds. Mutual funds with a sales charge, typically 8.5%.

M

M1. The basic measure of money supply, consisting of currency, demand deposits and other checkable deposits.

M2. M1 plus saving and small time deposits plus money market deposit accounts plus shares in money market funds.

M3. M2 plus large time deposits.

Management Fee. The fee charge by all investment companies for managing the portfolio. A typical fee is 0.5% of the net assets.

Margin. That part of a transaction's value that a customer must pay to initiate the transactions, with the other part being borrowed from the broker. The initial margin is set by the Federal Reserve System. The maintenance margin is the amount, established by the brokers and the exchanges, below which the actual margin cannot go.

Margin Account. An account that permits margin trading, requiring $2,000 to open.

Margin Call. A demand from the broker for additional cash or securities as a result of the actual margin declining below the maintenance margin.

Market Value. The market value of one share of stock is the current market price; for the corporation, it equals market price per share multiplied by the number of shares outstanding.

Money Market. The market for short-term, highly liquid, low-risk assets such as treasury bills and negotiable CDs.

Money Market Deposit Accounts. Accounts at banks and thrift institutions with no interest rate ceilings.

Money Market Mutual Fund. A mutual fund that invests in money market instruments.

Mortgage-Backed Securities. Securities representing an investment in an underlying pool of mortgages.

Municipal Securities. Securities issued by political entities other than the federal government and its agencies, such as states and cities and airport authorities.

Mutual Funds. The popular name for open-end investment companies. A mutual fund continually sells and redeems it own shares.

N

NASDAQ. The automated quotation system for the OTC market, showing current bid-ask prices for thousands of stocks.

National Association of Securities Dealers (NASD). A self-regulating body of brokers and dealers overseeing OTC practices.

No-Load Funds. Mutual funds that do not have a sales charge (load fee).

O

Open-End Investment Company. Any investment company whose capitalization constantly changes as new shares are sold and outstanding shares are redeemed.

Over-the-Counter (OTC) Market. A network of securities dealers for the trading of securities not on the exchanges.

P

P/E Ratio. The ratio of stock price to earnings, using historical, current or estimated data. This ratio is also referred to as the multiplier.

Par Value. The value assigned to a security when it is used. For bonds and preferred stock, par value is equivalent to face value. For common stocks, par value is arbitrary and of little importance.

Payout Ratio. The ratio of dividends to earnings.

Portfolio. The securities held by an investor taken as a group.

Preferred Stock. An equity security with an intermediate claim (between the bondholders and the stockholders) on a firm's assets and earnings. Dividends are specified, but can be omitted.

Premium. The amount by which a bond or preferred stock exceeds its par or face value. For closed-end investment companies, the amount by which the current market price exceeds the net asset value. In the case of options, the price paid by the option buyer to the seller of the option.

Primary Market. The market for new issues of securities, typically involving investment bankers.

Prospectus. Provides information about an initial public offering of securities to potential buyers.

Q

None.

R

Real Assets. Physical assets, such as gold or real estate.

Return on Assets (ROA). A fundamental measure of firm profitability, equal to net income divided by total assets.

Return on Equity (ROE). The rate of return on stockholders equity, equal to net income divided by equity.

Risk. The chance that the actual return on an investment will be different from the expected return.

S

Secondary Market. The market where previously issued securities are traded, including both the organized exchanges and the OTC.

Securities and Exchange Commission (SEC). A federal government agency established by the Securities Exchange Act of 1934 to protect investors.

Standard & Poor's Stock Price Indices. Market value indices of stock market activity, with a base of 10 (1941-1943). The S&P 500 Composite Index is a broad and well-known measure of market activity.

Stock Dividend. A payment by the corporation in shares of stock rather than cash.

Stock Index Futures. Futures contracts on stock indices, including the S&P 500, the NYSE Index, and The Value Line Index.

Stock Index Options. Option contracts on a stock market index such as the S&P 500.

Stock Split. The issuance by a corporation of a larger number of shares of stock in proportion to the existing shares outstanding. A split changes the book value and the par value.

Syndicate. Several investment bankers involved in an underwriting.

T

Technical Analysis. The methodology of forecasting fluctuations in the prices of securities, whether individual securities or the market as a whole.

Term to Maturity. The remaining life of a bond.

Treasury Bill. A short-term money market instrument sold at discount by the U.S. government.

Treasury Bond. Long-term bonds sold by the U.S. government.

U

Unbundle. The separating of brokerage charges so that customers pay only for those services desired, such as execution services.

Underwriting. The process by which investment bankers purchase an issue of securities from an issuer and resell them to the public.

Unlisted Security. A security not listed on one of the exchanges.

V

None.

W

Wealth. The sum of current income and the present value of all future income.

X

None.

Y

Yield to Maturity. The indicated (promised) compounded rate of return an investor will receive from a bond purchased at the current market price and held to maturity.

Z

Zero Coupon Bond. A bond sold with no coupons. It is purchased at a discount and redeemed for face value at maturity.

Editor's note: the glossary above is reprinted in part from: Charles P. Jones *Investments: Analysis and Management*, 2d ed. (New York: John Wiley & Sons, 1985, 1988), pp. 675-88. Reprinted with permission.

To Order Copies of This Book (Either Singly or in Quantity):

Call Meister Press / The Book Distribution Co-Op
Toll-Free: 888/98-BOOKS
or
SSS&A Investment Advisors, Inc.
Toll-Free: 800/424-5577

To Contact the Author:

Dr. Sherman S. Smith may be reached for
consulting, financial management,
speaking engagements, etc. at:

SSS&A Investment Advisors, Inc.
1836 Second St., Napa, CA 94559
Toll-Free: 800/424-5577